MAXIMIZING YOUR
FEDERAL
BENEFITS

*How to Understand and Use Your
Full Compensation Package*

AVIVA
PUBLISHING
NEW YORK

D1523161

Maximizing Your Federal Benefits
How to Understand and Use Your Full Compensation Package

Address all inquiries to:
Kevin Hocker
6209 Mid Rivers Mall Dr
Suite 290
Saint Charles, MO 63304
phone: 1-877-317-4167

www.fedbenefitsgroup.com

ISBN 978-1-890427-18-4

Library of Congress Control Number: 2009933580

Editor: Beverly Holloran & Morgan Chilson
Cover Design: Jeremy Henderson
Typesetting: Fusion Creative Works, www.fusioncw.com

Printed in the United States of America

For additional copies, visit: www.fedbenefitsgroup.com

Author's Note

This book was published with the goal of educating federal employees. It addresses important issues surrounding many aspects of your federal benefit package. We hope you will read it from cover-to-cover and embrace a new attitude toward your benefits and your retirement planning. We have covered a broad range of topics but this should never substitute your own investigation before making important decisions. We have taken painstaking efforts to condense, simplify and refine a rather complex topic and deliver it to you in the most useful manner possible. We hope *Maximizing Your Federal Benefits* will answer many of your questions and encourage you to find the ones it doesn't.

This publication is designed to provide competent and reliable information regarding the subject matter covered. However, it is sold with the understanding that the authors and publishers are not engaged in rendering legal, financial or other professional advice. Laws and practices often vary from state to state and if legal or other expert assistance is required, the services of a professional should be sought. Although the information has been gathered from sources believed to be reliable, please note that

Contents

It's all about YOU!

We live in very interesting economic times. Now more than ever, people experience sleepless nights, anxious paydays and tough budgeting decisions.

The world is changing so quickly, that we have little or no time to adapt. It seems almost daunting to balance a job, a marriage and a family with any real feelings of success. Sometimes it's all we can do to take care of the basics.

On top of that, as a federal employee, you must understand the full scope of your government benefits, figure out the right financial decisions and coordinate the details that will affect you today and, more importantly, into retirement? Good luck!

Many employees express that they are overwhelmed by their government benefits and have just given up trying to understand them altogether. They have many questions they can't seem to get the answers to. Questions like...

- When can I retire?

- How well off financially will I be when I retire?

- Am I taking advantage of all the federal benefits available to me?

- How soon is too soon, and how late is too late?

- Will I have enough money to retire?

- Are there any decisions I can still make that will impact my future?

- Am I making some mistakes (even if by omission)?

- I lost money in the TSP. Do I have enough time to recover?

- How much should I be putting in my TSP?

- Should I buy back my military time?

- What about Social Security if I retire before age 62?

- Can Medicaid effect my annuity payments?

- AND what's that number in the bottom right-hand corner of my pay stub???

You've got questions; we've got answers! Specifically, *Maximizing Your Federal Benefits* answers these questions – and many more – as they relate to you, first as an individual with dreams and goals and, second, as a government employee.

The timeless cliché, "What you don't know won't hurt you" may be true in trivial matters but it is certainly NOT true when it comes to your Federal benefits and retirement package. Each year employees forfeit hundreds of thousands of dollars in UNCLAIMED benefits. And they pay an even greater cost because of what they THINK they know that isn't actually true.

Whether you realized it at the time or not, when you started your federal employment, you entered into a partnership with the US government in regards to your retirement. There are a couple of ways we like to categorize this partnership.

1. Proactive versus Reactive and

2. Participant versus Spectator...

As with any partnership, both parties have certain responsibilities.

Getting the most from your retirement "partner" will mean taking an active part in understanding, interpreting and applying all the terms of your agreement.

This short book is not full of boring data about what you should "do." Rather, it's more about who you can "be." Become an active partner. Assume responsibility for your future. Make plans and set goals instead of watching days slide past on the calendar. This is YOUR life and YOUR future. It's all about YOU.

It has been said that 70% of the car is the driver. Well, we can tell you from our own experience with thousands of federal employees that it's not the benefit package you have which determines a successful retirement, but **what you do with that benefit package** that makes all the difference. There are not many situations where a driver gets in an accident and the car is to blame!

Our goal is to make you a better driver.

Beyond that, we'll help you maximize your benefits so you get the most out of them while you are working and, of even more concern, so you don't outlive them when you aren't.

So get behind the wheel. Start the car. Your first driving lesson awaits.

PART ONE:

Maximizing Your Understanding

CHAPTER ONE:

Be Where You Are

"Being content makes poor men rich; being discontent makes rich men poor." ~ **Benjamin Franklin**

We chose to include Ben Franklin's wisdom as a reminder to focus on the good as well as the challenging aspects of your government careers. In our work with government employees, we find many lose sight of what they really have within their careers, and that frequently there is true reason for contentment. We will explore that concept further in this chapter. So without further adieu, let us say:

"Congratulations, you work for the government!" And, of course, on certain days we can also say: "Our condolences, you work for the government!"

This is an unwavering theme we find with many employees. They are happy to have a stable government job, a fairly secure benefit package and a host of other benefits we will remind you of in a moment. Yet they are frustrated by the confusion surrounding those benefits that all too often turn "congratulations" into "condolences."

There is actually a short list of disadvantages employees complain about. These include:

- Strict procedures and processes they must adhere to.

- Frustration because they know more efficient ways to accomplish a task, but changing government procedures requires more time and red tape than the same change would require in a private company. A governmental solution to a problem is oftentimes as bad as the problem itself!

- Delayed promotions because employees tend to stick around longer.

- Co-workers don't pull their weight (or face repercussions).

Yet in the final analysis, most employees agree a government job provides a demanding, rewarding career path.

Despite the few disadvantages, working for the government is hard to beat. However, we all tend to take things for granted when we get used to them. (If you don't know what we're talking about, ask your spouse!)

It's only natural to consider the grass on the other side of the government fence just a little greener than our own. So if you have ever considered breaking away from the government, we invite you to revisit some of the facts that follow before you scout greener pastures.

Size (And Age) Really Does Matter!

The federal government has been operating for 226 years. We think you'll agree that's just a *little* bit longer than *most* employers!

With 2.6 million workers on its payroll, it's by far the nation's biggest employer. Annual revenues of $3.3 trillion demolish those of those other "mom and pop" shops like, say, AT&T and Microsoft.

The government also offers an unmatched array of opportunities, crossing the spectrum from nuclear physicist to postal worker, forest ranger to secret agent and even president of the United States.

Now, if all of *that* isn't enough to keep you committed to Uncle Sam, then let's take a look at some solid facts about why "congratulations" are in order for those of us with government jobs.

Job Security and Stability

Now more than ever, employees of even giant Fortune 500 companies like MCI, Enron and United Airlines live with the constant worry of becoming the victim of massive layoffs or even of watching their employers go out of business altogether. In recent years, brand-name industry icons most of us thought would be around forever suddenly shut their doors. Companies like Circuit City, Steak & Ale and Linens 'N Things, just to name a few.

Becoming a federal employee pretty much takes that constant worry about job security off the table. As long as the 285 million citizens of the world's most powerful and stable nation demand national security, interstate highways, consumer and environmental protection, an equitable system of justice and a long list of other essential government-provided services, Uncle Sam is in business. And, historically speaking, its annual growth has outstripped that of the U.S. economy as a whole.

Here's an equally important factor in assessing job security: in the absence of employment contracts, private employers can fire workers **at will**. That means private workers can be fired for no reason or even an unfair reason, as long as it's one that doesn't violate federal or state laws against discrimination on the basis of race, gender or age.

Federal workers enjoy a much higher level of protection against arbitrary or unfair job action or termination. They can be fired only for narrowly defined reasons: primarily, proven incompetence or dishonesty/fraud. And elaborate grievance procedures before an impartial board are available to federal employees to test the validity of any job action. If job security is important to you, Uncle Sam should be your employer of choice.

Competitive Pay

Uncle Sam is the only employer in the country required by law to pay workers at prevailing private sector wages. Under Title 5, section 5301, federal pay rates for white-collar employees are required to be competitive with private-sector pay rates for the same levels of work within the same local pay area. This is implemented by two types of annual pay adjustments: a general increase based on changes in the Employment Cost Index (ECI) and a locality pay adjustment based on variations in pay levels among 32 geographical areas.

A minority of the largest, most profitable private employers has been found to provide somewhat higher base pay than federal employees. But even there, the difference is typically less than 10%.

We ask you: is that enough of a pay hike to risk the rampant "job insecurity" found in the private sector?

Often that difference disappears or becomes reversed when you factor in the many types of incentives provided to federal employees, including locality adjustments, hardship differentials, cost-of-living allowances (for overseas duty), relocation bonuses, retention allowances, recruitment bonuses, incentive awards and student-loan repayment.

These additional forms of compensation can add up to **100% or more** of base pay. For example, a valued GS-13 grade federal employee working overseas might earn as much as $150,000 in some areas.

Generous Retirement Benefits

Federal workers enjoy the clearest advantage in the area of retirement benefits, according to a 1998 Congressional Budget Office comparison of the compensation levels of federal and non-federal workers.

For example, a 35-year-old federal worker with 10 years of service earning $45,000 in annual salary would accrue a whopping 51% more in retirement benefits for the year than his private-sector counterpart ($5,320 vs. $3,516). Another example: a 55-year-old with 20 years of service earning a $75,000 salary would accrue 31% more in retirement benefits ($14,435 vs. $10,998).

What makes this retirement differential even more meaningful in this day and age is the fact that federal employees can transfer their credit for years of service between the federal government's many branches and agencies. A former Army officer can tack on his 6 years of military service should he become a federal civilian employee. (Try getting credit for your 6 years at Microsoft if you leapfrog to Apple!)

Furthermore, federal employees can accrue considerable retirement security at a relatively young age. It's not unusual for a federal employee to retire at age 55 and receive 80% of what he was earning during the average of his three highest-earning years.

Generous Vacation Time and Holidays

Do you enjoy time off with the family? Then you're in luck: federal workers enjoy about 20% more paid vacation time and holidays than employees in big private companies. A new federal worker earns 4 hours of vacation time for each 2-week pay period, or 13 vacation days per year.

After 3 years, vacation time accrues at the rate of 6 hours per pay period, or 20 days a year. A federal employee with 15 years of service earns a generous 5 weeks of paid vacation time per year. Remember, that's in addition to the 10 paid holidays guaranteed to **all federal workers**.

Competitive Health Insurance Benefits

You often hear private sector employees grousing about their insurance, driving halfway across town to the dentist for a checkup. That's not the case for federal government employees.

In fact, federal employee health insurance benefits are structured to provide less coverage than those of large private-sector employers during an employee's working years but dramatically more during retirement years.

A 35-year-old federal worker in 2008 with 10 years of service earning $45,000 a year would receive $3,265 in health insurance benefits per year, 5% more than the $3,106 of his private-sector counterpart. For a 55-year-old making $75,000 annually, health insurance benefits would total $5,410 per year, 2.8% more than the $5,265 for his private-sector counterpart.

Generous Sick Leave and Disability

All federal employees accrue 4 hours of sick leave for each 2 weeks worked. Sick leave can be used to care for close family members. The Family Medical Leave Act provides for up to 12 weeks of time off (using accrued leave or leave without pay) per year for medical emergencies.

Sick leave may be accumulated from year to year. This sick leave accumulation is intended to be your short term disability coverage. By comparison, federal workers' sick leave and disability benefits exceed those of private-sector employees by about 10% across the board.

It's been said that if the grass is greener on the other side, it is probably receiving better care. But if you're a federal employee who thinks the greener grass resides in the private sector, there's a good chance you just quit looking at the beautiful lawn growing in your own backyard. Hopefully, this quick walk through your benefits helped you see it all over again.

CHAPTER TWO:

We Must Unlearn Before We Learn

For your convenience, this book is divided into two parts. Why? Well, it has a little something to do with "teaching an old dog new tricks." Specifically, before we teach you anything new, most of you will need to "unlearn" some things you thought you already knew. As they say, it doesn't do any good to wax a dirty car. If you do, then you just keep the dirt in place even longer!

Therefore, the first part of this book will be running you through a "mental car wash." This will clean off the "dirt" of misconceptions, misinformation and misunderstandings. We will then dry you off and apply a clean, shiny coat of wax (knowledge) so you'll be ready to take to the fast lane of understanding and utilizing – or should we say, "Maximizing Your Federal Benefits!"

In the upcoming chapters we outline what we call **Patriotic Principles**. These are principles that, if followed, we believe will make you a more productive employee, allow you to create a more successful career and enjoy a more fulfilling retirement as you learn to maximize your many benefits by simply understanding what you already have.

Okay, if you had any doubts about whether you wanted to retire from the government, Chapter 1 should have straightened you out! So let's start looking at things a little differently and, better yet, managing life and making decisions from that perspective.

Even if you do end up leaving the government before you retire, what you will learn in this book will allow you to maximize the time you do spend with the federal government and learn how to turn that experience into a gold mine for future use, personally or professionally.

In the Introduction, we mentioned that 70% of the car's performance depends on the driver. Let's take a closer look at what we mean by that and how it relates to you.

We are sure you know two different employees who are on opposite ends of the financial spectrum, even though they earn about the same and have the same benefits package. How is it that two people with the same starting line (income and benefits) wind up crossing the finish line so far apart?

Well, it could have a little something to do with these thoughts:

The Truth Will Set You Free

Our inspiration to write this book came from our shocking experiences over how much confusion, lack of understanding and misunderstanding came out of the mouths of the federal employees who we talk to in our line of work.

We have been to many seminars, conventions and private appointments where what the employee *thought* was correct and what was *actually* correct were literally worlds apart.

So how do you rank? What are your various myths about the federal government, and how do they compare with the truth? Below are examples of misconceptions we hear frequently.

See if you know the answers:

1. The TSP is matched 15% if you are in management. (**True or False**)

2. If you want to cancel your FEGLI, you need to wait for an open enrollment. (**True or False**)

3. Open enrollment for FEGLI is once a year. (**True or False**)

4. If both you and your spouse are covered through the government health insurance and your spouse dies, the HR department will automatically reduce your premiums to reflect a single individual. (**True or False**)

Trust me, these are a mere sampling of what we have come across in our talks with federal employees. So, how did you do? The answers are:

1. False

2. False

3. False

4. False

It's okay if you got a few right, got a few wrong or even got all of them wrong. This book will dramatically improve your score the next time around!

You Are Responsible For You

The lack of understanding and confusion about your benefits is not isolated to one area. In other words, if we could merely teach you on this benefit or that one, this book would be much shorter – and your road to understanding much quicker!

Instead, the depth of misunderstanding and confusion is endemic across nearly all departments and also within various areas of your benefit package. However, we can assure you it is not the fault of the government, your supervisor, OPM, personnel or anyone else. The first lesson we want to convey in this chapter is that **you are responsible for you**.

Now, we don't mean to come across as rude or insensitive. This is reality. The culture of many federal employees is "our benefits are confusing so we will just trust that everything turns out all right;" rather than "if I were to take more of an interest in my benefits, research them a little more, I might be able to understand them better."

See, you *can* be responsible for you.

Now, in regards to what we are about to share with you, we are not contradicting the idea that you are responsible for yourself and your benefits comprehension. But we believe it is worth a little commentary on the history of your retirement systems to help move that understanding along a little. As most of you know, 1984 brought a change in the retirement systems.

A Change Is In the Air

The original retirement system was called CSRS, or the Civil Service Retirement System. This system paid employees a guaranteed pension if they met certain requirements (age, years of service, etc.).

Employees didn't have any additional responsibilities to ensure a pension. They still had life insurance and health insurance that they needed to understand, but at least the pension was handled. Whether it was enough to retire on was based on the lifestyle of each employee.

Then, in 1984, the government introduced FERS, or the Federal Employee Retirement System. In this system, many of the benefits stayed the same. However, the annuity to the employee is where the significant changes occurred.

A typical 30-year career employee who was hired under FERS would receive about 20% less through his or her annuity. The 20% cut would need to be made up through the TSP and Social Security. We will get more into those aspects in a later chapter. For now, we want to stay consistent with our comments about what we see happening in the system today.

Avoid Advice from "The Others"

Many federal employees admit they don't understand their benefits all that well. However, with or without a general understanding of those benefits, they are faced with decisions about many important things.

Most of these decisions are made based on what others are doing, and most of what others are doing is based on what others did. Here is the problem with the "others." (And no, we are not talking about the people in the TV series *LOST*.)

When you listen to the "others," here is what you'll often find: an old-timer Civil Service person will give opinions about what is the best fund to be in with the TSP, or when to move money, etc. He or she will tell you how much life insurance you need, etc.

They Don't Send Ducks to Eagle School

The problem with **general advice** from "the others" is that there is no **general situation**; everyone and every situation is unique, even in the federal government – perhaps especially in the federal government, where a wide variety of cultures, socioeconomic classes and personality types mingle on a daily basis. The only thing about federal employees that is the same is their benefits. Everything else is full of variables.

For example, here are a few of the many variables that make advice from "the others" less than accurate when it comes to you being responsible for you:

- Date of hire

- How many years an employee will work
- How much an individual puts in the TSP
- The income of a spouse
- The retirement of a spouse
- The amount of private investments
- The amount of personal savings
- Inheritance
- The number of dependents
- Lifestyle preference
- Debt
- Spending habits
- Life expectancy
- Spouse's life expectancy
- Spouse's insurance
- College expenses
- Equity in home
- Inflation when YOU retire
- Tax bracket (current and future)
- Future income needs
- Risk tolerance
- Which phase you're in (we will explain in a later chapter)

- Elderly parental support

- Health (now and at retirement)

- How many years you are able to work

- Return % on contributions

- And so on and so on…

So What about Bob?

Many times, we hear from employees that the reason for their current benefits decisions was because "Bob" said it was best. Bob who? Who, exactly, is Bob? What retirement system is he in? How do any and/or all of the above variables come into play? When did Bob get certified as a financial planner and in which state is his broker's license?

I mean, aren't these things you'd ask of a "real" financial adviser?

So why aren't you asking them about Bob?

The real problem we have found with Bob and his ilk is that much of the advice that is floating around out there is rooted in older school, CSRS employees (because they were the first ones who walked the earth) who don't have the same responsibilities (not to mention variables) as FERS employees.

Regardless of its actual merits, "Bob" is innocently trying to help and offer free advice. However, the most expensive advice is free advice! Unless "Bob" is a financial advisor or an expert employee in the personnel department, we urge you to be cautious.

The 3 Main Phases of Life & Retirement Planning

Let's not blame Bob for all of our financial woes. Remember, only you can truly be responsible for you. Let's increase both our responsibility for – and our understanding of – federal employee benefits by more closely examining the three main stages of life and especially retirement plans:

Accumulation Phase: We accumulate the most assets in our earning years. This is when we are working full-time, socking money away (hopefully), investing in stocks and bonds, putting money in our 401(k) or IRA accounts and, hopefully, paying off our mortgage.

Preservation Phase: As retirement draws near, we focus less on accumulation and more on preservation; we take fewer risks with stocks and bonds and put more in trusted bank CDs, annuities and other slow but safe investments. We tidy up loose ends to protect our homes, our cars and other assets.

Distribution Phase: After accumulation and protection, we turn our thoughts to distribution. How will we turn our pensions, TSP and other assets into income that we won't outlive?

Ask yourself these types of questions: What phase am I in? What phase is my money in? How can I be in the same phase with my money?

In future chapters we will get more specific about how to accumulate, protect and distribute your assets, but let's turn our attention to something you need to understand before we can do any or all of the above.

Let's move on to the Patriotic Principles...

CHAPTER THREE:

Patriotic Principles

When it comes to understanding your federal benefits, it helps to paint by numbers. Specifically, there are 6 **Patriotic Principles** for Surviving the Federal Retirement System, which you should know and understand:

Patriotic Principle #1: *Retirement -- It's Exactly What You Make it*

Many employees have put in a lifetime of government service expecting their retirement will take care of itself through their pension, Social Security and TSP contributions (if applicable), and because of a deep belief that the government they serve will take care of them. Unfortunately, it's usually not until retirement that they discover the four built-in traps waiting for federal employees who accept the "default" retirement plan:

1. They have huge and unexpected tax liabilities.

2. The FEGLI life insurance schedule becomes unaffordable and leaves the vast majority of them under-insured at the time of need.

3. The investment options for the TSP retirement funds are LOW RETURN or HIGH RISK.

4. Nearly all federal employees are painfully under-funded in retirement.

We've already touched a little on Patriotic Principle #1, but we will now go a little deeper to intensify your understanding. The number one reason people don't live a life they want is because **they don't take responsibility for it**.

For whatever reason, nature or nurture, simplicity or naiveté, certain people blame someone or something for their conditions or circumstances. On the other hand, happy, successful people are people who take responsibility for their own lives regardless of what obstacles and challenges may come their way.

We know how much easier it is to blame, deny or even hide from your responsibilities; it's human nature to bury our heads in the sand and hope everything will just go away. Unfortunately, while our minds might work that way, our problems don't. In fact, it's been said that you can dodge your responsibilities, but you can't dodge the **consequences** of dodging your responsibilities.

This first Patriotic Principle is the foundation of everything else. After all, if you don't take responsibility for you, then none of the other principles to follow will do you any good anyway.

There are many successful people in the world, federal employees and otherwise, who had more disadvantages than you did but, one way or another, found options to make things work. The difference in their success can be traced directly back to responsibility.

So from this point forward we don't want you to ever let the little voice in your head tell you anything different or allow you to make any excuses. Are your benefits confusing? Is life busy with not a lot of extra time? Are you a single parent? Are you in debt?

There are a million things that can stand in the way of you being responsible for your life, but you aren't going to let any of them distract you from personal accountability any longer. You are going to find ways around them, over them and through them… and we are going to help!

Federal employees who adopt this positive, responsible mindset and make a decision to get their financial lives (and many other parts) in order are suddenly smarter, definitely more empowered to figure out what they need to know and, consequently, learn what they need to do to set things up the way they want. Many people have reported incredible peace of mind after embracing Principle # 1 because they took the first step – taking responsibility.

Patriotic Principle #2:
Only One Economy Matters -- YOURS

In many of our seminars, employees approach us wanting to know what they should do with their TSP. They ask us what funds they should be in and if they should move their money into the "G" fund; others want to know how much FEGLI they need, etc.

Of course, our goal is to deliver good information and provide answers to their questions. However, we think Einstein made an excellent point when he said, "I never teach my pupils. I only attempt to provide the conditions in which they can learn."

Do you remember Bob from a few pages back? Well, we don't ever want to become a Bob. Many of the questions we are asked don't have a "right" answer. The answer usually depends on a number of things going on in the employee's life at the moment, as well as variables mentioned before.

In other words, there is no cookie cutter response we can give to the complex, game-changing questions we're often asked. What might be a good decision for one employee would be a bad one for another, and vice versa. That is why it is crucial you embrace the first principle. In this chapter, we want to show you where to aim some of that responsibility you have. If we have any goal at all, it is not to give information; it is to inspire people to seek it.

In all things, we want you to remember one driving philosophy: *"Manage your mind before you manage your benefits."* That is why when people ask us for tips on managing their TSP (or whatever they are asking about) we tell them they are skipping a step; before they manage their TSP, they need to manage their minds.

Your bank account and almost every other aspect of your life have more to do with what is going on between your ears than anything else in your external world – and that's especially true of what's going on between both sides of your wallet!

Let's start with the concept of two economies:

1. The general economy

2. Your economy

You don't have much control over the general economy (the bank bailouts, income tax codes, a recession or depression), but you *do* have control over your own economy. This is evidenced by the fact that there are people doing just fine financially in what is considered a tough economy, and there are people who do poorly in the best of economic times.

Somebody will always cite that Boogeyman known as "the economy" as a negative factor in good times or in bad, in busts or in booms. Try to think of the economy as neutral. Your attitude and thoughts about the economy are what make it so. We know it is not the economy that determines a successful career or retirement, but rather a philosophy.

We realize that if you watch 5 minutes of the news (actually, it only takes 5 seconds) you can conclude the world is in pretty bad shape these days. But just as you have complete control to change the channel on your TV, you also have control to change the channel in your head.

The economic times we are experiencing are actually exciting times for many people, but only for the people who are **watching a different channel**. If you look at history you will find amazing statistics and revelations that should give you hope about the future.

The news will tell you that, from an economic standpoint, we are in the second Great Depression (or Depression 2.0, as it's now being referred to). Well, we don't know about you, but we didn't live through the Great Depression. Though, we do know what came after it.

Since that 10-year stretch, there were many people who thought the world as they knew it was over. But consider our current society. Walk through a mall, an electronics store or drive a late model car. We have Laptops, software, GPS, the World Wide Web, email, cell phones, space shuttles, digital cameras, iPods, text messaging, wireless headsets, Bluetooth, Blackberrys, iPhones, microwaves, HDTV, DirecTV, You Tube and the newest Lexus can parallel park itself. Names like Facebook and Twitter couldn't have been imagined by the greatest forecasters. (We could go on and on.) If this is the kind of stuff that is produced AFTER an economic hardship, then we want to make sure we don't miss out!

In fact, the Great Depression (despite its negative connotation) spun quite a few successful things out of its web. Here are just a few companies that were either started or began thriving during the gloom and doom: *Readers Digest, Time* magazine, *The New Yorker*, Walt Disney and Mickey Mouse, The Boeing 247 and the Douglas DC-s, Pitney Bowes, Betty Crocker, The Band Aid, Caterpillar Tractor, A&W Root Beer, the bagel, Gerber Product, Mrs. Stovers, Pan American, Rotor Rooter, State Farm, Kleenex, Avon, The Blue Cross concept, Clairol, Revlon, Hostess, Wonder Bread, Dolly Madison, White Castle, Hewlett-Packard, Kellogg's, Post, Proctor & Gamble, Chevrolet and Camel Cigarettes.

Radio and print media grew significantly, and The FDIC and SEC were formed. This is but a fraction of the good things that took place during – and after – the Great Depression. In other words, to those hardwired to see doom and gloom, any boom time can be a depression. To those who recognize change as opportunity and realize progress comes from hard times, any recession can be a boom.

Happy, sad, good times, bad times, pretty, ugly, rich or poor; it's all in your mind. One of our mentors, Jim Rohn, always says it like this when asked about the next ten years, "It will probably be pretty much like the last ten. We will have opportunity mixed with adversity and adversity mixed with opportunity." What a great assessment!

We've got to get out of our minds and into our lives, and start working at it instead of worrying about it. Don't complain because your neighbor's house is bigger or Bob's retirement account has more dollars in it; get out your brochures, crunch the numbers, make some changes. Get out of your head and into the real world where real change occurs.

It was the famous Earl Nightingale who uttered these words, "If the grass is greener on the other side, it's probably getting better care." Don't envy your neighbor's lawn. Take better care of your own!

The road to career success and retirement success doesn't start with your benefit package, your life insurance selection, your savings account or your Thrift Savings Program. It starts in your head.

Patriotic Principle #3:

Long-range Success Starts with Long-range Thinking

We met with a man in his early 20s who had just finished his first year with the Post Office. As with many young people who are establishing homes and families, retirement was far from a top priority to him. But as we projected his financial future over the next 40+ years, it became clear to him that he could make small decisions now to greatly impact his future. We set up a tax-free Roth IRA at $50 a paycheck. He didn't know where he was going to come up with that kind of money, but knew that it was the right thing to do.

A couple of paychecks later, I called him and asked if he could increase it by $5. He agreed. Two paychecks later, I called again, and again we raised it by $5. He continues to increase the deduction each month. Five dollars may not seem like much, but at that rate, in less than three years he will be putting $5,000 per year into his Roth, and he'll still be less than 30 years old! Because of the guaranteed interest account we were able to get him into, and the many years he will benefit from the miracle of compound interest, he will retire with nearly one MILLION dollars of tax-free money.

In Proverbs we read a lot about wisdom. "Happy is the man that findeth wisdom, and the man that getteth understanding." We are even told it is better to get wisdom than gold. Ben Franklin said an investment in knowledge always pays the best interest.

Many of us ignore wisdom because we liken it to knowledge, education, college degrees or other types of "book learning," but in fact wisdom is little more than experience dressed up as understanding.

Wisdom is looking around, seeing the way the world should be, recognizing what needs to be done to live a fruitful, righteous, blessed life and then doing it. Without excuses (which are unwise), without cheating (which is un-righteous) and without waste (which is un-fruitful).

Wisdom is knowing you should be saving... and doing it; wisdom is knowing you need to understand your benefits better and understanding them. The wise are not always sexy because, let's face it, it's more fun to go hit happy hour with the gang than sign up for that after-work seminar on your TSP or G Fund. But when you know it needs to be done, when someone is making it easier for you to do it, what is the wise choice?

Patriotic Principle #4: *Knowledge is Money*

Have you ever started a diet? What's the first thing you do when you get up on the morning of Diet Day #1? You weigh yourself, right? It's not fun, it's often rather traumatic – particularly if you haven't done so in awhile – but it's the first step if you want to be successful. Why? Well, how would you ever know how much weight you lost if you didn't first know how much weight you needed to lose?

Or how about this scenario: imagine going to a sporting event where they not only didn't keep score, but there wasn't even a clock to let you know how long the game was going to last. How would you know if you were winning or losing? Furthermore, would you even care that much about how you played the game?

Numbers are how we keep score; figures are how we face facts. When it comes to understanding and utilizing your federal benefits, let us offer two critical statements:

1. You can't improve what you don't measure, and

2. The reason people don't get what they want is because they don't know what they want.

How much do you have? How much do you need? How much are you contributing? Does it add up? These are all questions that can act as guides as we move forward in this critical process of maximizing your understanding to maximize your benefits.

Although, like stepping on a scale it might not be pleasant at first, a simple self-examination and financial check-up could make the difference between a stressful retirement and a comfortable one.

The good news is this doesn't have to be a complete overhaul of your benefits nor do you need a Ph.D. in finance to understand them all. Oftentimes, a very minor adjustment or level of understanding is all you need to make big changes that produce big results.

Think about golf for a minute, which is appropriate since we're already talking about retirement. Just a minor tweak in where you hit the ball makes a big difference in where the ball ends up. You don't have to murder the ball to get it where it needs to go. Golf, like finance, is a game of finesse, of minor adjustments, or attention to the tiny details.

Many people just need little tweaks to make big differences. The problem is they think it is the other way around, so they ignore everything and play the avoidance game because they think it will be too painful to look at and deal with it.

Let's talk about organization for one minute. We want to talk about how important clearing out the past can be for building the future. What causes many people to procrastinate in the first place is they are not used to completing things.

Think about all the half-starts, false-starts and big-starts we make in our lives; the closets full of board games and puzzles we were going to use on those "family nights" that never caught on, the garage or basement full of gym equipment that we now use as expensive clothes hangers because that "fitness kick" never quite kicked in. We are experts at starting but oftentimes failures at following through.

Many times we don't complete things because we are unorganized (mentally and physically). For example, many people have unbalanced checkbooks, cluttered garages, clothes from 5 years ago they don't wear, junk drawers, a Sanford and Son basement, stacks of unfiled papers, photographs in plastic tubs instead of those fancy, elaborate, coffee table worthy albums we keep meaning to buy.

What turns a principle like Patriotic Principle # 4 into a belief is action; and with action you, too, can get organized and truly read all those benefits manuals, updates, newsletters and memos you've been storing!

It's not too late, you know. No matter how far off from – or close you are to – retirement age, you need to begin not just saving for retirement, but also being responsible for it, even if you have debt and little or no savings. Savings, benefits and retirement aren't about the size of the investment but the regularity of the habit.

Even if you don't have a dime saved up, start now. Think about where you'd be today if you'd started saving five years ago. Better still; think about where you'll be five years from now if you start today!

Patriotic Principle #5: *JUST DO IT!*

We are a country full of extremes; either we do it all or we don't do anything. Either we lose 50 pounds or we gain 55; either we are obsessed with saving or completely negligent about our checking accounts.

Utilizing your federal benefits effectively is not an all-or-nothing exercise; it's a matter of compromise, understanding and attuning yourself to the details. In other words, you don't need an oil change every day and you don't need to go 80,000 miles without one. By taking the time to learn about your benefits and acquiring some "wisdom," you can then spend minimal time managing things without ignoring them to your own detriment.

Procrastination is a particular evil we visit upon ourselves merely by putting things off until, quite often, it is far, far too late.

For instance, when was the last time you went to the ER without a firm understanding of your benefits – until you got the bill later and had to call two dozen numbers to get a straight answer? Reading a simple brochure on a lazy Sunday morning could save you hours of heartache – and hundreds of dollars next time you need medical help.

Last year we were working through the retirement paperwork with an employee who had accumulated over $500,000 in his TSP account. In that state at that time, we were able to show him an annuity that would have paid him a 12% bonus up front ($60,000!), an 8% bonus the second year (an additional $44,000) AND pay him more than $2,500 each month for life while continuing to grow the principle.

Though he had already spent many months researching, he said he "needed to think about it." We talked with him recently, and he still has his $500,000 in the TSP. His balance is unchanged from a year ago. His indecision (the paralysis of analysis) has already cost him well over $100,000. Sadly, the bonus program is no longer available in that state.

Zig Ziglar use to talk about getting "cooked in the squat" while waiting for… the holidays to be over, to lose some weight, to have more money, for the kids to leave home, etc. The story comes from a childhood memory in which Zig peeks in the oven at some biscuits that failed to rise. When asking the cook what happened, she laughed and replied, "Well, those biscuits squatted to rise, but they just got cooked in the squat." In other words, they were going to rise but just never got around to it.

Don't get "cooked in the squat." Don't wait for the holidays to be over, the weight to be lost, the kids to be gone, the money to pile up before you act with responsibility toward your many federal benefits and understand how they will affect you in your very near future!

Patriotic Principle #6:

Set a Course and Keep a Roadmap Handy

Change is the only constant.

Doesn't that make you feel just a little better about change? I mean, think about it: as much as we like to treat change as this great big surprise-like thing that pops into our life from time to time, our lives change on a daily basis, and change IS really the only constant.

We get up every morning with one thing in mind. By the end of the day, the constant, little, miniscule, ever-present changes of modern life – the conference call that took too long, the traffic you didn't expect, the line at the dry cleaners, the kids' soccer practice that you forgot all about – take us in another direction altogether.

To deny change, which is in effect almost hourly every day, is to be unprepared for change when it inevitably occurs. The best way to face change is to welcome it, embrace it and, above all, expect it. Because when it's all said and done, if you don't handle change, change will handle you.

Your benefits change over time; they accumulate, restructure, reorganize and, inevitably, mature. To keep pace with how your benefits are changing, you must adapt to change and embrace it.

There are many benefits to change, but not if we fear it, dread it and try mercilessly to avoid it. Looking back on our lives, isn't it true that some of our most rewarding experiences – a new job, a new home, a relocation, a new child, a new pet – were those changes we initially resisted? Think of how different our lives might be if, instead of fearing change, we welcome it and see it for the opportunity it really is.

Very frequently, we encounter employees in their late 50's or early 60's who are carrying the full FEGLI insurance of 5 times their salary: $250,000 – $300,000 in life insurance in addition to their free Basic Life.

The reality is that in many cases they simply don't need that much insurance anymore. The mortgage is paid, the kids are through school and living on their own, they have enough in savings to cover final expenses, and yet they're paying $200 - $400 each month for insurance they don't need! Life changes, and as it does, so do your financial needs and priorities. A regular inventory of needs, goals and investment tools could save you thousands of dollars over your lifetime.

PART TWO:

Maximizing Your Benefits

CHAPTER FOUR:

The Good, the Bad and the FEGLI

We're going to talk now about your FEDERAL EMPLOYEES GROUP LIFE INSURANCE, or FEGLI. Life insurance is a crucial part of your benefits package, and we believe you need to thoroughly understand this most important coverage.

FEGLI coverage is available to all career employees. Let's start by helping you determine what coverage you have by interpreting the FEGLI code on your check stub.

The FEGLI code begins with the letters IN followed by a number, a letter (or number 9) and then a number. The number following the IN indicates your age group, and the corresponding rates for each insurance:

    1 = under 35

    2 = 35-39

    3 = 40-44

    4 = 45-49

    5 = 50-54

6 = 55-59

7 = 60-64

8 = 65-69

9 = 70 and over

The next letter, or number 9, indicates which options you have elected.

A – Ineligible

B – No Benefits

C – BL

D – BL, A

E – BL, C

F – BL, A, C

G – BL, Bx1

H – BL, A, Bx1

I – BL, C, Bx1

J – BL, A, C, Bx1

K – BL, Bx2

L – BL, A, Bx2

M – BL, C, Bx2

N – BL, A, C, Bx2

9 – BL, Bx3

P – BL, A, Bx3

Q – BL, C, Bx3

R – BL, A, C, Bx3

S – BL, Bx4

T – BL, A, Bx4

U – BL, C, Bx4

V – BL, A, C, Bx4

W – BL, Bx5

X – BL, A, Bx5

Y – BL, C, Bx5

Z – BL, A, C, Bx5

BL = Basic Life   A = Option A   B = Option B   C = Option C

The final number, 0, 1, 2, 3, 4 or 5, shows the number of units selected with Option C, if any. If you did not elect Option C coverage, this will be a zero.

NOTE: Since Postal workers receive Basic Life coverage at no charge, their pay stub may not have an IN code if they did not elect any additional optional coverage. The Basic Life coverage will appear on their annual Statement of Benefits, though it does not appear on the pay stub.

Basic Life Insurance Coverage

First, is the Basic Coverage. As we mentioned, Postal workers get this coverage at no charge. All other branches pay $0.15 per $1,000 of coverage. Basic Coverage is calculated using your Base Pay. You can calculate your Basic Coverage by taking your

Base Pay

Round it up to the next thousand

Add $2,000 and that equals

Total Basic Coverage

Consider this simple example. Joe has a base pay of $45,300. His Basic Coverage would be:

$45,300 (Base Pay)

$46,000 (Rounded Up)

<u>+ $2,000</u>

$48,000 Total Basic Coverage

As you get pay raises and COLA's, your Basic Coverage will also increase. You use the exact same calculation, with your new base pay after each raise.

Your Final Expense Benefit

Your Basic Life Insurance includes a little-known and seldom-claimed final expense benefit. If you retire prior to age 65, your Basic Life Insurance will remain in effect until age 65. For the next 38 months, it will reduce by 2% each month until the benefit reaches 25% of the original amount. Example: If Joe earns $52,000 at retirement, his Basic Insurance coverage is $54,000 until age 65. Over the next 3 years and 2 months, his coverage will reduce each month until it reaches $13,500 (25%).

Here's the part most federal employees don't know about: this coverage stays in effect FOR LIFE! Because most employees and their beneficiaries are unaware of this "final expense" benefit, it is almost never claimed. To take advantage of this added benefit, inform your Executor and your beneficiaries of this information. Put a note with your will, final papers and insurance documents. Beneficiaries should call the Retirement Information Office at 1-888-767-6738 for assistance.

Extra Benefit

Your Basic Coverage has an additional feature called the Extra Benefit. The Extra Benefit is basically a Bonus on your Basic Coverage for being under the age of 45.

Employees who are under the age of 45 will get a multiple of their Basic Coverage depending on their age.

The ages and the applicable multiples are listed below:

35... 2.0	39... 1.6	43... 1.2
36... 1.9	40... 1.5	44... 1.1
37... 1.8	41... 1.4	45... 0.0
38... 1.7	42... 1.3	

Let's look at an example to show you how the Extra Benefit would work. Let's take Joe again who has a Basic Coverage of $48,000 from our previous example.

Let's also assume Joe is 38 years old, which qualifies him for the Extra Benefit. Joe's Extra Benefit would be calculated by taking his Basic Pay and multiplying that amount by the Extra Benefit Factor of 1.6 from our previous chart:

Basic Life Coverage: $48,000

Extra Benefit Factor: x 1.6

Total Basic & Extra Benefit: $76,800

It's important to understand that when Joe turns 39, his Extra Benefit will be reduced to 1.5 and continue to reduce as he gets older until he turns 45 and will have no Extra Benefit. The current insurance company who has the life insurance contract through the government is willing to give you this additional Extra Benefit at no cost because you are younger and less likely to pass away.

For all federal employees, the Cost of Basic Coverage is $0.15 per thousand dollars of coverage. An employee with $50,000 of Basic Coverage would pay $7.50 a pay period for that insurance. Remember, Extra Benefit insurance is at no additional cost.

Living Benefits Act

The next area of your FEGLI coverage is the Living Benefits Act. Very few federal employees are aware of this part of their benefits, but it is a critical subject and worth covering.

The Living Benefits Act was passed in 1995. It was intended to benefit employees diagnosed with terminal illnesses. Under the Living Benefits Act, if an employee is diagnosed with a terminal illness and has 9 months or fewer to live, the employee can access his or her full Basic Coverage plus any applicable Extra Benefit at the time of diagnosis.

This coverage allows ill employees to receive their benefits while they are living. This valuable coverage can allow employees to spend their final days with family and spare their loved ones the financial concerns that often accompany a terminal illness.

Unfortunately, this coverage is very rarely used because most employees are unaware of this option. Please make your loved ones aware of this valuable coverage and if you have co-workers who could use this coverage, bring it to their attention.

Optional Insurance

Options A, B and C each add a different benefit to the FEGLI package. Employees can choose to add these when they are hired. These benefits may be reduced or cancelled at any time, but can only be added or increased during an "open season" which OPM occasionally offers, or following a "qualifying event" such as marriage, divorce or birth of a child.

OPTION A

This coverage is something you elected to pay for when you were hired. Option A is a very straight forward coverage under your FEGLI. It provides a $10,000 death benefit to beneficiaries in the event of the employee's death.

Like most FEGLI insurance, the price does increase every 5 years, but because the coverage is so small, the cost is usually not an issue. Some employees refer to this coverage as a very affordable burial policy.

OPTION B

Option B within your government life insurance is very popular among federal employees. This option allows employees to take anywhere from 1 all the way up to 5 times their base pay in additional life insurance if they choose to pay for it. In most cases, this decision is made when the employee is hired.

A simple example would be if Joe has a 50,000 base salary and he took 5x Option B he would have an additional $250,000 of life insurance coverage. The cost of this coverage is based on your age. The government devised the plan and pricing. A list of prices per thousand dollars of insurance coverage (rates effective as of January 1, 2003) is listed below in the first two columns. The second two columns show the rapidly increasing costs per paycheck for an employee making $50,000 and choosing the option B x 5 option.

Age	$/thousand	cost	$/pay period
Under 35	$0.03	$250,000	$7.50
35-39	$0.04	$250,000	$10.00
40-44	$0.06	$250,000	$15.00
45-49	$0.09	$250,000	$22.50
50-54	$0.14	$250,000	$35.00

55-59	$0.28	$250,000	$70.00
60-64	$0.60	$250,000	$150.00
65-69	$0.72	$250,000	$180.00
70-74	$1.20	$250,000	$300.00
75-79	$1.80	$250,000	$450.00

As you can see from the chart, rates increase as you age. They don't increase very quickly until age 50, and then things get pretty nasty, pretty fast. The reason they increase the cost is because the employee didn't have to take a physical to get this additional coverage. The only thing the insurance company knows about you is your age, so that is the basis they use to increase coverage. As you get older, you are more likely to pass away so they charge you more and more.

*Special Note: If you are healthy and do not have a family history of illness it is almost always a better plan to look for life insurance in the private sector. Almost any insurance plan you find in the private sector will provide a level death benefit and level premiums as well.

For example, using rates available in the private sector today, a healthy 40-year-old male will pay $250 in annual premiums for $250,000 of coverage and that price will be locked in for 20 years.

Under FEGLI rates, to get that same $250,000, a 40-year-old employee will pay $390 in annual premiums for 5 years, $585 each year for the next 5 years, $910 per year between the ages of 50 and 54, and a whopping $1,820 each year from 55 to 59 years of age. At age 60, under the current FEGLI rates, that amount will more than double.

Currently, in the private market, a healthy 50-year-old male can lock in rates for 20 years on $250,000 for annual premiums of around $625.

As a general rule, if you are healthy you are better off getting your life insurance with a private company and protecting yourself from the increases the federal program allows. If you are unable to obtain approval from a private company, keeping the federal life insurance until you cannot afford the price may be your best option.

Very few people in the federal government understand the details of their life insurance program. The cost of not understanding how the program works can cost the employee thousands of dollars in premiums they wouldn't have paid if they had known what you just learned.

If you just figured out that you may be paying too much for your federal insurance, check and see what a private company could do for you in terms of a replacement policy. Those of you who would like our assistance can contact a Benefit Specialist through our website www.fedbenefitsgroup.com. Our comparison quote allows us to shop 14 different companies for you and ensures you have the best price available given your situation.

OPTION C

This is your Family Coverage provision, and is an optional coverage you elect to pay when hired on with the government. Family Coverage is life insurance on your family where you will be the beneficiary should something happen to your family members.

Family Coverage is offered in units. An employee can take 1-5 units of Family Coverage. Each unit represents $5,000 on your spouse and $2,500 on each dependent child. Dependant children are unmarried children under the age of 22, and unmarried foster and adopted children living with you in a parent-child relationship under the age of 22.

Let's look at an example of an employee who took 5 units of Family Coverage. With 5 units, the spouse will be covered for $25,000 and each dependent child will be covered for $12,500.

It is important to note that there is no limit to the number of dependent children covered under your Family Coverage. Another important aspect of Option C is you cannot "drop" part of the coverage. For example, if your dependent children leave you cannot drop the coverage on your children and keep the coverage on your spouse. When it comes to Family Coverage, you either have it or you don't.

CHAPTER FIVE:

Thrift Savings Plan (TSP)

The Thrift Savings Plan (TSP) was implemented as part of the Federal Retirement benefits package and serves as a vehicle to accumulate retirement funds. Though technically it is NOT a 401k because it falls under the direction and control of Congress, for the purpose of understanding how it works, it shares most the plusses and minuses of all other 401k plans.

On the plus side, in 1984 when the FERS program was started, Congress established 5% matching funds for FERS employees as an incentive to encourage retirement savings. This is one of the best programs in the country, and provides FREE MONEY to FERS employees for their retirement.

The government will contribute 1% of a FERS employee's salary to their TSP fund whether they choose to contribute or not. (This is separate from the FERS retirement fund, and is vested after 3 years.) They will also match the first 3% of an employee's contributions dollar for dollar, and 50 cents for every dollar of the next 2% the employee puts in, making a total of 5% government funds to match the first 5% of an employee's contribution.

These are funds you cannot make up later, so it is beneficial to maintain a 5% contribution to the TSP right from day 1 of eligibility. Over a career, a FERS employee will build a nice nest egg by establishing this pattern, and allowing the government to give them a 100% return on this money.

Unfortunately, the TSP also shares in the weaknesses that have surfaced in the 401k concept.

First, it was originally designed as a tax shelter, but has never been as effective as intended. In a 401k, taxes are deferred on contributions while an employee is working and are assessed as income when the funds are withdrawn during retirement. The theory was that this would be at a lower tax rate, thereby creating a tax shelter on both the contributions and the earnings.

Right from the beginning, the tax savings have been minimal. The cost of living has steadily increased, as has the standard of living, so not only do things cost more in retirement, but people want and have more. While pensions and Social Security checks are significantly less than their paycheck while they were working, adding a spouse's retirement income and taking withdrawals from savings will frequently result in an end-of-the-year tax bracket that is similar to pre-retirement rates. And those rates continue to climb. In fact, most 401k funds that are withdrawn in retirement are assessed at an equal or higher tax rate than they would have paid when they were deposited. Most retirees experience NO tax savings through 401k income, and will see as much as one-third of their funds lost to taxes.

Second, until an employee reaches the age of 59-1/2, 401k funds are inaccessible without penalty or interest. Don't kid yourself. Until you pay taxes on that money, it's not your money!! If it was your money, you could use it whenever and however you wanted. But because taxes have not been paid, the IRS regulates those funds very carefully. If you withdraw funds prior to age 59-1/2, you must pay a 10% penalty plus count the withdrawal as income for the year, and pay taxes accordingly. Or you may BORROW the money (from yourself) and repay yourself with interest! (Interesting that the government is not required to guarantee you interest while THEY have control of the funds, but if YOU have the money, you MUST pay interest or be assessed the penalty and taxes...)

On a positive note, a unique feature of the TSP plan set up by Congress for federal employees is that if you retire from federal service prior to age 59-1/2, and have not paid a penalty for a previous withdrawal, you may roll your TSP funds into a qualified plan without penalty. The sooner you exercise this option, the quicker you can control your tax liability. Contact Federal Benefits Group prior to starting your separation paperwork to make sure you understand your options.

The third problem with the TSP is that the investment options it offers are very low return or very high risk. The past few years point out the dangers of tying retirement funds to the market. If you are a federal employee, you're well aware the vast majority of your co-workers LOST money in their TSP after October 2007. Many lost more money in 2008 than they earned in wages during the same period! Those who didn't lose were primarily in the G fund and gained around 3%. Remember, one-third of that will be taken out in taxes, so the resulting gain will be slightly less than the cost of living increase over the same period. In other words, even at its best, in a down market, the TSP produced a zero or negative return on investment.

Fourth, the TSP has an enormous tax liability. Taxes will have to be paid on every dime of contributions and interest. And in event of the premature death of the employee, those taxes can be at the highest assessed rate! The 401k has proven to be a windfall for the government to collect taxes when an employee dies leaving money in the account. In this unfortunate event, the entire balance is distributed to the beneficiaries and charged as income for the year. This means that a surviving spouse may now be one of the "wealthy Americans" who will pay maximum tax rates. It is not Bill Gates and Warren Buffet who end up paying higher taxes. It is every American with a 401k and every federal employee with a TSP account who will be penalized when they least expect it.

And finally, many employees are depending on their TSP as their only supplement to Social Security and their pension. Virtually everyone who does this will be required to take a pay cut in retirement. Even with the matching funds, 5% savings is not enough to build a retirement income equal to their previous paycheck, especially if those investments rise and fall with the market. While most people know they should be saving more, very few do, and unmatched funds in the TSP are subject to the disappointments of the low-return / high-risk options.

HOW MUCH IS ENOUGH TO PUT AWAY FOR RETIREMENT?

The answer to this question will vary according to every individual's needs in retirement. Generally speaking, if we start before age 30 and invest 10% of every dollar we make until age 65, we will retire at an equal or better income than we're accustomed. If we wait until after age 30 to start saving, we will need to put away 12-15% to reach that same level. And if we're over 40, we may need to put away 15% or more to build a comfortable retirement income.

A WINNING STRATEGY BY A LETTER CARRIER

The example below is courtesy of a very prudent employee who shared her formula with us. Every employee has unique circumstances, and yours may be different. However, her experience outlines how she made the most of her TSP investments, never exposing them to risk while getting a predictable and positive outcome.

"As a FERS employee, I have always contributed 5% to the Thrift Savings Plan. Since the government matches my 5% with another 5%, I figure I'm making an immediate 100% return on my investment. Since I'm not an expert in investing, and don't know too much about the market, I've kept my money in the "G" fund, where it doesn't lose anything. I know it's not exciting or sexy, but I figure I've already doubled my money, and I never have to wake up in the morning and wonder how much I've lost while I was sleeping. On my salary,

5% is just a little over $100 each pay period, or about $2,700 per year. My contribution plus the matching funds from the government plus the interest on the whole balance helped my TSP account grow by almost $6,000 last year while most my co-workers were losing thousands of dollars. I don't plan to retire for another 13 years, and at this rate I'll put in around $35,000 in contributions. With the matching funds and modest interest, my TSP will grow by another $100,000. With the other money I'm investing, I'll have enough for retirement."

Learning from her example, saving $5,000 per year at 2-5% interest will accumulate around $150,000 in a 20-year career. That can add $1,000 or more in monthly income during retirement, and go a long way toward filling the income gap most employees face when they leave their job.

To learn more about some of the specific things this employee did, and other options that may make sense for you, and to speak with a Benefit Specialist in your area, contact us at www.fedbenfitsgroup.com. We have seen many employees who were managing the EXACT same benefit plan as another employee and yet one employee had to get another job at retirement while one retired from the government with more income than they made while they were working. There are many GUARANTEED INTEREST and TAX-FREE funds available that most federal employees are unaware of.

For the federal employee making $52,000 / year, 10% means putting $200 per bi-weekly paycheck toward retirement. If you are like most employees we talk to everyday, you are over 30 and have not started budgeting the full amount necessary to secure your future. Perhaps you are among the thousands of people starting over because of bankruptcy, divorce, refinance, kids, failed business ventures, health issues or a hundred other reasons. Or maybe you're like me, and just never thought you'd get old!

The good news is, in most scenarios we deal with, THERE IS HOPE. The hard news is, you will have to get both aggressive and smart about your retirement investments. Without taking food off the table or shoes off the kids' feet, you must begin the process of adjusting your current budget to find $100 or $200 or even $300 per paycheck *over and above* the 5% matching contribution to the TSP, and invest it regularly and wisely. A Benefit Specialist can work with you to see if you qualify for one of the ZERO-risk, high-interest savings plans on the market, (yes, they DO exist!) and what other options may fit your specific situation. You may get more information at www.fedbenefitsgroup.com.

CHAPTER SIX:

Here's to Your Health!!

Flip a coin. Roll the dice. Pick a card, any card. Unfortunately, that's how most federal employees choose their health plan.

Each year during open season for health benefits, every federal employee has an opportunity to investigate their health benefit options. Although benefits change within the plans, and premiums continue to increase annually, many federal employees leave their health insurance choices to chance, and never look at a plan other than the one they're in. This may be because they're happy with their plan, or it may simply seem too overwhelming to consider looking at other choices. In this chapter, we'll simplify the process of comparing health plans by breaking down how to compare and understand the various plan choices.

First, some simple rules that apply to all plans:

- During open season which is typically the second Monday in November through the second Monday in December, federal employees and retirees may enroll in, change or cancel their existing health plan. They can also choose to enroll in, change or cancel their dental and vision coverage. And in order to participate in the flexible savings account for the following year, employees must state how much they want to contribute for the year.

- All federal health plans are required to have a "no pre-existing condition" clause. This allows federal employees to move from one plan to another during open season each year without worrying about any existing health conditions. Each plan must take your enrollment no matter what your health condition. This continues even when you are retired.

- Each plan also is required to have a maximum out-of-pocket limit for the year. If you reach that limit, you will not be required to pay any further expenses, including co-pays and deductibles due to this limit. The amount of the out-of-pocket limit varies from plan to plan, so you'll want to be sure you understand what the maximum amount you could have to pay out of your own pocket is for the plans you are considering.

Some handy definitions:

FEHB – Federal Employee Health Benefits

FEDVIP – Federal Employee Dental and Vision Insurance Plan

PCP – Primary Care Physician

FSA – Flexible Savings Account

HSA – Health Savings Account

HMO – Health Maintenance Organization

PPO – Preferred Provider Organization

FFS – Fee-For-Service Plan

HDHP – High-Deductible Health Plan

IOU – What you use if you don't have good insurance

E-I-E-I-O – Catchy tune to sing in the Dr's office

CHOICES, CHOICES, CHOICES.

Traditional types of health plans

HMO – Health Maintenance Organization. This is coverage where you choose a primary care physician from a list of member physicians to provide your general health care. Any visits to a specialist must be referred by your Primary Care Physician (PCP.)

There is typically no coverage for out-of-network care with the exception of emergency care. You are not required to pay a deductible, but there are often co-pays associated with office visits and prescriptions.

PPO – Preferred Provider Organization. This is a group of contracted providers who you can select from. You do not have to name one particular provider to be your primary care physician and can visit any doctor as long as they are on the preferred provider list. These plans vary by state with many different options available around the country.

You are not required to stay within the network, but the insurer will pay more if you do. Typically, your insurance company might pay 80% and you would pay 20% if you went to someone on the preferred provider list. If you went out-of-network, the insurer might only pay 70% and you would have to pay 30%.

There are usually deductibles required each year and also expect to pay co-pays which are often larger than in an HMO.

FFS – Fee-For-Service. The fee-for-service plans are offered nationwide and all federal employees have access to them. The line between a PPO and a fee-for-service plan is fairly blurry. Like the PPO, you can choose your provider from an approved list. Your reimbursement is normally 80% of covered expenses which are considered reasonable and customary – as determined in the contract between the provider and the insurance company.

Comparing an HMO to a PPO or FFS, you have less flexibility and more restrictions in an HMO which results in lower premiums, but possibly higher out-of-pocket expenses. The more choices and control you have, the more it costs you.

Should you choose a traditional plan? Much of this decision is driven by how healthy you and your family are. Your health will be a guiding factor in choosing the best coverage for you.

Traditional coverage is designed for people with fairly significant health issues. If you have a chronic condition, see a specialist more than 3 times a year, are on several on-going medications, then a traditional plan may be for you. Although there are usually higher premiums associated with traditional plans, you'll also stand to have more of your health expenses covered during the year. As with all of the health plans offered through FEHB, there are annual out-of-pocket maximums that limit how much you would have to pay in any given year.

Consumer-driven health plans

These are recommended for those who have fewer health issues than those mentioned for traditional coverage. You might have a minor ongoing condition such as allergies or acid reflux for which you take one or two prescriptions occasionally. If you see a specialist, it might only be once or twice per year. Consumer-driven health plans typically have a set amount of coverage that they pay before you are required to pay anything – a reverse deductible if you will. As an example, the insurer might pay the first $2,500 in expenses on a family's coverage. You would then be responsible for the next $1,500 and then the insurance company would pick up 90% of the charges and you would be responsible for 10%, up to an out-of-pocket maximum of $6,000.

Any amounts you do not use out of the insurer's first $2,500 can be rolled over to the next year – provided you stay in the same health plan. So, if you only needed $2,000 of coverage this year and stayed in the same plan, next year, the insurer would pay the first $3,000 of your expenses ($500 from this year + $2,500 for next year). These plans are for those who are generally healthy.

HDHP – High-deductible health plans. A high-deductible health plan is a fairly new offering for the federal government. Less than 2% of federal employees are enrolled in these plans. We believe this is not because they are not viable options, but because employees simply don't understand the benefits.

If you do not have any known medical issues and only go to the doctor for routine physicals or the occasional flu, and you don't have any ongoing prescription needs, this might be a great choice for you.

A high-deductible health plan can be expected to have lower premiums with higher deductibles. For any of you who remember what they used to call catastrophic insurance where you only had coverage for a major health event, but you could afford to pay for other day-to-day health care expenses - that is essentially what a high-deductible health plan does.

HSA – Health Savings Account. The high-deductible health plan comes with a health savings account (HSA). The HSA associated with the high-deductible health plan is different from the flexible savings account (FSA) it is often compared to in that you do not have to use all of your funds each year. The biggest complaint about the FSA is that it's use it or lose it. The HSA funds roll over from one year to the next – regardless of whether you stay in a high-deductible health plan or not.

Another difference is that the HSA funds earn tax-free interest where flexible savings account funds do not. We'll talk more about FSAs later in this chapter.

The funds are completely portable meaning that if you retire or leave federal service, the funds are yours to take with you and spend on health care expenses in the future. The custodian of the HSA will provide you with a debit card which you can use to pay deductibles, co-pays and other health-related expenses. You can continue in a high-deductible health plan in retirement until you reach age 65 and become eligible for Medicare.

The funds you accumulate in your HSA during your working years can be utilized for health care expenses in retirement –

including premiums on your federal employee health benefits after age 65. The HSA acts as a healthcare IRA. The funds are even inheritable by your heirs!

How do you get funds into your HSA? There are two ways. The first is to contribute funds each month. This can come directly out of your checking account to go – pre-tax- into the HSA. The second way is that the insurer gives back a portion of the premium you pay directly into the HSA. That's right. You receive a rebate from the premiums you pay, actually reducing your overall health care costs.

You must be in a high-deductible health plan to have an HSA. The only exclusions from participating in the HSA are:

- You cannot be enrolled in Medicare.

- You cannot be enrolled in a non-OPM health plan.

- You cannot have accessed benefits through the VA in the past three months.

- You cannot be enrolled in Tri-Care or Tri-Care for Life, and

- It will limit how you can participate in an FSA (you can't contribute to the FSA for health care expenses, but you are still allowed to use the FSA for dental and vision.)

Some common expenses you can pay out of your HSA include:

- Out-of-pocket expenses like deductibles and co-pays,

- Dental expenses,

- Vision exams, contacts, glasses,

- Hearing aids and batteries,

- Chiropractors,

- Acupuncture, and interestingly,

- Qualified long-term care premiums.

Using the HSA's tax-free capabilities is the *only* way to get a federal tax break on your long-term care premiums.

SO WHAT'S THE DIFFERENCE?

We've talked about types of plans and how your health can help determine your best option, but what about things like levels of service and how much control you have over your own healthcare? The following chart shows four areas you should consider when making your decision.

	HDHP	PPO/FFS	HMO
Red Tape/ Paperwork	Lots	Some	Almost None
Emphasis on Keeping You Out of the Hospital	Cost incentives	Pre-approval	Non-hospital treatments first
Choices of doctors, hospitals and other providers	Some are network only; others pay something for out-of-network	In network reduces costs; Out-of-network providers increase costs	Must use in-network providers; no coverage for out-of-network
Use of Case Management	Limited	Limited	Substantial

- In terms of paperwork and the "hassle" factor, an HMO is the easiest to deal with, while the high-deductible health plan involves more paperwork and pre-authorizations, etc.

- Cost containment – emphasis on keeping you out of the hospital which is the most expensive place to receive care – varies dramatically, as well. The high-deductible health plan provides incentives to the plan participant to take responsibility for their care, while the PPO and Fee-for-service plans require pre-authorization and the HMO endorses non-hospital treatments if possible before choosing a hospital solution.

- All three types of plans require you to utilize their preferred providers to different degrees. It's your responsibility to understand what is required by the plan in order to avoid unnecessary out-of-pocket expenses for yourself.

- Each of the high-deductible health plans and the PPO/FFS have limited case management capabilities. This means you will be responsible for managing more of your overall health care. If you're having surgery, for example, you'll need to be sure that not only the hospital and surgeon are on your insurer's preferred provider list, but that the anesthesiologist and any other medical professionals who might consult on your case are on that preferred list, as well. The strength of HMO's is their case management ability. You don't have to worry about whether a specialist is on a preferred provider list because if your primary care physician has referred them, they have to be within the system. This is done to contain costs.

WHAT$ THE BOTTOM LINE?

Speaking of costs, how important is cost to you? Of course, we all want to pay as little as possible for health insurance, but is it your most important factor? While you are working, your share of the insurance premium is paid with pre-tax dollars – called premium conversion. Once you retire, you no longer receive this benefit and must pay your premiums with after-tax dollars. The federal government continues to pay their proportionate share – approximately 72% - for both you and your spouse even after retirement. This is one of the best benefits you get for your years of public service (other than your annuity). Your spouse can continue on your coverage as long as you live, but if you want to ensure that their coverage continues even if you pass away first, you'll want to be sure and take a survivorship benefit on your federal annuity for them. This election at retirement allows you and your spouse to be covered by federal health benefits as long as you both live with the federal government paying 72% of your premium and you paying 28%!

Often two federal employees will be married to each other and each take self-only health coverage. The premiums for two self-only policies are less than family coverage. This seems like a cost-effective plan. However, keep in mind that each employee has to meet the plan's maximum out-of-pocket limit if they're under two separate plans. This is particularly of interest as employees/retirees age and tend to have higher overall health care expenses.

You are eligible to continue your health benefits in retirement as long as you retire on an immediate annuity and have been enrolled in the FEHB for at least five years either as an employee or family member. You do not have to be enrolled in the same health plan the entire five years, but continuously enrolled in any FEHB plan.

A common misconception is that your spouse has to be enrolled for five years prior to your retirement. This is NOT true! As long as your spouse has other coverage, they can enroll in your plan either after a life-changing event (such as retirement) or during any open season. A pitfall to avoid here is that if your spouse continues to work after you retire and keeps their own health coverage, thinking they'll get on your plan when they retire, if the federal retiree passes away before the spouse has a chance to retire – the spouse loses the access to those health benefits (because they were not covered by the FEHB at the time of the retiree's passing). Even if you take the survivor benefit to enable your spouse to continue health benefits if you pass away first, if the spouse is not covered by FEHB on the day you die, they are unable to get FEHB coverage.

Your overall health care expenses include more than just your share of the premium. You also have to take into consideration what your maximum deductibles could be, as well as any co-pays for doctors, hospitalization, and prescriptions. In the case of the high-deductible health plan, you also get a rebate from the insurance company, so you get to deduct that amount from your overall expenses.

Look at the following illustration comparing out-of-pocket expenses for an employee insuring self only:

Self Only	HDHP	Standard
Limit stated in Plan's Summary of Benefits	$5,000	$4,500
Deductibles	Included	$350
Hospital, Physician, Drug Co-pays	Included	$2,560
Specialty Drug Limit	Included	$4,000
Premium Minus Savings Account	$88	$1,992
Actual Limit to You	$5,088	$13,402

As you can see in this illustration, it's possible to pay much higher expenses in a standard level plan than the high-deductible health plan, especially if you have to meet the full deductible in each plan.

DENTAL AND VISION

In 2006, the federal government added separate dental and vision benefits to your health benefit offerings. Some health plans include a small provision for dental coverage, but it is usually limited, so you might want to have additional coverage, as well. The coverage is available to all current and retired federal employees through FEDVIP. It is offered on a group basis which reduces the cost of the premiums, but the government does not subsidize any portion of the premium.

One of the issues with the FEHB is that you must choose between self or family coverage. If you are married with no covered children, you pay the same amount as the person in the cubicle next to you who is married with four children. The dental and vision programs allow you to choose between self only, self + one, and self and family to make the premiums fairer.

As in the health plans, pre-existing conditions are covered, although you'll want to check the limitations for things like orthodontics, crowns and bridge work. You also get to pay your premiums with pre-tax dollars just like your health insurance. You can choose just dental, just vision, both or neither.

NOTE: You do not have to be enrolled in the FEHB to participate – although you must be eligible for the FEHB.

The dental and vision coverage are the secondary payors if you have coverage under your FEHB. As an example – if available, your health coverage would pay first, then your FEDVIP coverage and finally if you're enrolled in the FSA, you could use those funds to pay any remaining amounts due.

When comparing dental benefits, you're looking to find the best coverage, that used in combination with your health coverage and FSA, will provide the most benefit for you and your family.

FSA – FLEXIBLE SAVINGS ACCOUNT

The Flexible Savings Account is not actually part of your health insurance coverage, but the open season is the same as the health plans. You must re-enroll and choose your contribution amounts to the FSA each year. You may contribute up to $5,000 each year in pre-tax dollars to be used for health expenses. Depending on your tax bracket, this effectively allows you to get a 20% - 40% "discount" on health-related expenses because you are paying for those expenses with pre-tax dollars. You can use the funds to pay medical expenses such as co-pays, deductibles, dental and vision care and prescription and non-prescription drugs.

Remember, your ability to contribute to the health portion is limited to use for dental and vision care if you are enrolled in the high deductible health plan and the HSA.

You can also set aside $5,000 in pre-tax dollars to pay for dependent care for children under the age of 13 and parents or other relatives dependent on you for their care and listed on your tax return.

The biggest complaint about the FSA is that if you don't use your contributions from the previous year by March 15 – you lose them. You can drive down the street early in March and in any Walgreens you'll see the signs "Spend your FSA $ here" If you have funds left, you can spend them on band-aids, Advil, contact lenses and solution among other things.

You can get more specific information on how your FSA dollars can be spent at www.fsafeds.com.

FINAL CONSIDERATIONS – CHOOSING YOUR PLAN

If you're going to compare the health plans available in your area, you'll want to start by choosing from the HMO/PPO/Fee-for-Service options and choose which one or ones you want to look at. Can you live with the limits of an HMO? If you want a little more control, you might move toward a consumer-driven health plan or a high-deductible health plan. How healthy are you and the members of your family? Do you have any specialist needs? Remember, the healthier you are (fewer ongoing medications, less specialist visits), the more attractive the lower-cost options of the consumer-driven and high-deductible health plans become.

You'll also want to consider what health services are important to you. Think about well child check-ups, chiropractic care, mental health, emergency services, preventative screenings, and hospitalization. There are probably only a few of these services that are important to you, and these needs will change over the years, which is why you'll want to review your health coverage at least every three years.

The plan documents that outline each insurer's coverage can be intimidating. Although they are supposed to make choosing a plan easier, they often serve the opposite purpose. They appear overwhelming and as a result, many employees simply stay with the same plan from year to year without evaluating whether it's still the best coverage for them.

But take a closer look: OPM did a great thing for you in terms of the plan documents. Any insurer who provides coverage under the federal health plan must organize their plan documents in the same format. This means all the plans will have similar features in approximately the same place in each document.

For instance: Any plan changes are documented in section 2. Even if you don't plan to change health plans, you should always look at this section for the plan you're currently in, so you're aware of any changes to the plan for the upcoming year. Detailed benefit descriptions always appear in section 5. You'll look here if you have a chronic condition and want to see exactly how it's handled. A summary of all plan benefits always appears in section 11.

A list of useful resources appears on our website at www. FedBenefitsGroup.com.

MEDICARE

We'll close out this chapter with a short primer on Medicare and how it integrates with your federal employee health benefits. One of the most common questions we hear is what to do about Medicare and my federal employee health benefits when I turn 65.

There are four components to Medicare:

Medicare Part A

Medicare Part A is the hospitalization coverage portion of Medicare and is free to anyone who has paid into the Medicare system for at least 40 quarters (or ten years). Because all federal employees were required to begin paying into Medicare in March of 1986, even if you're in CSRS, you should be covered here.

Because it is free to you – you've paid in 1.45% while you're working – you'll want to sign up for this coverage at age 65. Your FEHB insurer wants you to sign up as well, because it helps take some of the burden off them.

You'll sign up for Medicare Part A when you turn 65. You have a 7-month window -that's three months before your 65th birthday, the month of your birthday, and three months after your 65th birthday to enroll. Whether you're still working or not, you'll want to sign up for Medicare Part A, because you do not pay anything for this coverage. If you are still working at age 65, your FEHB will remain the primary payor until you retire, when Medicare will take over as the primary payor.

Medicare Part B

Medicare Part B has a cost of $96.40 per month and if you opt for this coverage at age 65 (or when you retire, whichever is later), it becomes your primary insurer and your FEHB acts as a Medicare Supplement. If your modified adjusted gross annual income is greater than $85,000, your premium increases on a sliding scale. This is known as "means testing." If you have the means to pay more – you're charged more for Medicare Part B.

Many federal employees question whether they need Medicare Part B. Keep in mind that unless you're turning 65 soon, much of what you're reading here could change by the time you get there. The general pros and cons of choosing Medicare Part B are as follows:

On the positive side, you'll have broader access and stand to have a greater portion of your health care expenses paid for. If you're in an HMO within your FEHB, you won't have to worry about those out-of-network costs being covered. Medicare would pick that up.

If you choose Medicare Part B, you will pay at least $96.40 more per month in premiums (in addition to your then-current FEHB premiums). Health care expenses for a couple enrolled in Blue Cross Blue Shield would be more than $7,000 per year before you've ever gone to the doctor! If you're healthy, you could save about $2,300 per year by simply keeping your FEHB only.

The downside of Medicare is that if you choose Medicare Part B, Medicare becomes the primary payor (they pay the first dollar expenses). Having Medicare become the primary payor means that you have to go to a physician who accepts Medicare. Many physicians are no longer accepting Medicare because it is a time-consuming process to file the paperwork which results in lower payouts than the typical insurer would pay AND it often takes longer for Medicare to pay them. You may also have to give up the physician you've gone to for years if you choose the Medicare Part B option. Unfortunately, more and more doctors are not taking Medicare.

If you are already retired when you turn 65, the rules are the same for enrolling in Medicare Part B as for Part A. However, if you are still working at age 65, you do not have to make the Medicare Part B decision until up to 8 months after you retire. If you do not enroll during this timeframe, you may still enroll during any open season which runs from January 1 to March 31 each year. However, you will incur a 10% penalty for each year past the enrollment deadline. You'll want to carefully evaluate your Medicare Part B options at age 65, so hopefully, you won't have to re-consider it in the future. The 10%/year penalty increases your premium permanently.

Because most federal employees are satisfied with their FEHB coverage, they simply keep that coverage at age 65 leaving the Medicare maze to others.

Medicare Part C

Medicare Part C is also known as Medicare Advantage and acts like an HMO for Medicare participants. You must have Medicare Part A and Part B to participate in Medicare Part C.

Medicare Part D

Medicare Part D is the prescription drug program enacted by President Bush in 2003. Depending on the prescription drug provisions of your FEHB, you may not need this coverage. As long as you have some prescription coverage within your FEHB, you are allowed to pick up Medicare Part D during any open enrollment without a penalty.

SUMMARY

As complicated as this part of your package may seem, understanding your options here can save you thousands of dollars over your career and into retirement. The government health plan is among the best in the country because of the variety of options you have to choose from each year, and the fact that they subsidize your premiums by 72% FOR LIFE! You can see what an important benefit the FEHB provides in your overall benefits and retirement package.

CHAPTER SEVEN:

The Reality of Retirement

This chapter will discuss the basic mechanics of the three retirement systems (CSRS, Civil Service Offset, and FERS) and address two questions we get asked the most that relate to federal retirement:

1. Should I buy back my military time?

2. What is the number in the lower right-hand corner of my paystub?

CIVIL SERVICE

CSRS employees were hired prior to January 1, 1984, or had at least 5 years of CSRS service and returned to work between the years of 1984 and 1987. A Civil Service employee could fully retire at age 55 with at least 30 years of service. If the employee worked past the 30-year minimum, he or she could earn a higher annuity (pension) in retirement. With 40 years of service, CSRS employees could earn as much as 80% of their average high three consecutive years of base pay as a pension. The CSRS employee pays 7% of his or her income toward CSRS retirement.

CSRS employees did not pay into Social Security. Those employees who earned their 40 quarters of Social Security credits prior to their federal service or by working a second job could earn a Social Security check on top of their pension checks. However, because of the Windfall Elimination Provision, their Social Security checks would be cut in half. The government viewed a CSRS employee as "double dipping" by getting a full pension and Social Security from the government. This provision has been challenged by CSRS employees but as of today it is still in effect.

One important choice or option the CSRS employee has pertains to the Survivor Benefit. A Survivor Benefit is a benefit paid to an employee's surviving spouse in the event of the employee's death. A CSRS employee can elect as much as 50% of the employee's pension check as a Survivor Benefit. This election will reduce their monthly check by 10% while they are living, and pay 50% to a surviving spouse for the remainder of their lifetime. They can also select any amount smaller than 50% and will see a corresponding reduction in their pension check depending on what they choose.

There are instances where the employee's spouse will not need a Survivor Benefit. Maybe the spouse has a pension of his or her own and the employee wants the largest pension check possible. In these instances, they can elect (0) survivor benefit. If they elect this option, the spouse will have to sign and notarize forms within the retirement package confirming this decision.

One important thing to keep in mind when electing Survivor Benefit as a CSRS employee is health insurance. An employee's spouse is eligible to maintain health insurance in retirement as long as the employee elected a Survivor Benefit for their spouse. This means if an employee does not elect a Survivor Benefit, they will not be eligible for health coverage under the federal health plan.

CSRS employees who want the health coverage for their spouse, but also want the biggest pension check they can get, should elect a $3,600 annual Survivor Benefit. This election will allow the spouse access to health coverage, but the annual amount is so small it will have a very minimal effect on the employee's pension check.

With $3,600 annually there is enough of a check coming to the spouse to cover the health insurance premiums. In the event of the employee's death, it is much easier on the spouse if the pension check will cover the cost of the health insurance preventing the spouse from having to remember to write a check each month.

A retiree may elect LESS than $3,600 annually. We only suggest that amount as what is needed to help cover health insurance costs.

CSRS/OFF-SET

CSRS/OFF-SET employees are employees who had 5 years of federal service prior to 1983, separated for at least one year and then returned to federal service in 1984 or later. The government required every federal employee after 1984 to pay Social Security. Because of this requirement CSRS/OFF-SET was created.

We will not bore you with the details but try to help you understand how it affects your pension check. CSRS/OFF-SET is a

CSRS employee. The only difference is you pay into Social Security and the regular CSRS doesn't.

Let's look at an example. If Joe retires at age 55 with 30 years of service as a CSRS/OFF-SET employee, he will receive the full 56.25% pension that is allowed for a normal CSRS employee. When Joe turns 62 and becomes eligible for Social Security his pension check will be "offset" by his Social Security check.

Pension check at 55...$2,125.00

Social Security Check at 62.............................$1,000.00

Retirement Income at 62:

Pension Check...$1,125.00

SSI Check...$1,000.00

Total Retirement at 62....................................$2,125.00

In a nutshell, you get the exact same monthly income as a regular CSRS employee. The only difference is at age 62 the income will come from two sources instead of one.

FERS

Employees hired Jan. 1, 1984, and after are FERS employees. Many people ask us why a second retirement system was created. No one will ever know the entire reasoning behind the government's decision to change systems. However (and with no judgment on our end), we will show you how FERS works, and you can make your own deductions as to the motivations behind the creation of this system.

FERS employees pay very little toward their retirement compared to CSRS employees. The CSRS employee paid 7% toward retirement where a FERS employee will only pay .08% (not even 1%) toward retirement.

It is also important to look at the differences in pension amounts between a FERS and a CSRS employee. A CSRS employee after 30 years and at age 55 will earn a pension check for life of 56.25% of their highest three years of salary. A FERS employee will only earn 30% after 30 years of service and reaching their minimum retirement age. We have listed the minimum retirement ages with 30 years of service below:

If you were born before 1948	55
In 1948	55 and 2 months
In 1949	55 and 4 months
In 1950	55 and 6 months
In 1951	55 and 8 months
In 1952	55 and 10 months
In 1953-1964	56
In 1965	56 and 2 months
In 1967	56 and 6 months
In 1968	56 and 8 months
In 1969	56 and 10 months
In 1970 and after	57

You can also retire with less than 30 years of service and your minimum retirement age with:

20 years of service at age 60 - 20% pension (1% per year of service)

5 years of service at age 62 - 5% pension (1% per year of service)

FERS employees pay into Social Security as well. Social Security is the second piece of the FERS retirement plan. One thing you may notice about the FERS retirement system is you are eligible to retire at ages under 62 before you would be eligible for Social Security. How can FERS employees afford to retire without getting their Social Security checks?

The answer is the FERS Special Supplement. Very few employees are aware of this program which is unfortunate. The FERS Special Supplement is money every FERS employee needs to know about.

Let's look at Joe, a FERS employee. He is retiring with 30 years of service at age 56. He is not eligible to draw Social Security until age 62. Under the FERS Special Supplement he is entitled to receive a check from the Office of Personnel Management equaling 75% of whatever his Social Security benefit would be at age 62. If Joe's age is 62, his Social Security benefit is $1,200, his FERS Special Supplement would equal $900. Joe would get this check from age 56 to age 62. Once Joe becomes eligible for Social Security, the supplement is stopped and Social Security starts sending his normal check.

WARNING: *It is very important that the employee understands you have to reach your minimum retirement age and either*

30-years of service or age 60 with 20 years to qualify for the special supplement.

Some agencies are offering Early Out's. If you have not met the minimum retirement age and years of service, you will not get the supplement. This can make a significant difference in your evaluation of taking an Early Out or not.

Should I Buy Back My Military Time?

In most cases, the answer is YES! Unless you are receiving a military retirement pension or insurance benefits, you should consider buying the time. The cost of doing so will usually be covered in less than 2 years by the increased pension amount.

FERS employees with military service BEFORE 1/1/57 will receive credit for their military time for annuity computations and no buy-back deposit is required. The FERS deposit is 3% of basic pay plus a variable market rate interest may be charged. Military deposits must be completed before you retire.

For example, let's say Joe served 4 years in the Army. At $10,000 per year, his base pay totaled $40,000. Buying this time back will require a deposit of 3%, or $1,200 plus any applicable interest. This can be done in a lump sum or arranged to be taken through payroll deductions, as long as it is completed prior to retirement. Adding 4 years of service will add 4% to his FERS retirement pension.

Since Joe's high-three salary is $50,000, 4% will add $2,000 per year to his retirement pension, or $167 each month. That will repay Joe's buy-back deposit in only 8 months. As a general rule, all honorable active duty military service is potentially creditable under FERS.

What is the number in the lower right-hand corner of my paystub?

This is the amount you have contributed to your retirement. CSRS employees contribute 7% of each check, while the FERS employees put in .08% of their pay. You will find the bi-weekly amount on your paystub next to the Retire (#) designation. This amount accumulates all year and is added to the total at the bottom of your paystub each January.

Here's what you need to know about this money:

1. You are guaranteed to get it back in retirement.

2. You have paid taxes on it when it was taken out, so it will be tax-free when it is given back.

3. You have an option to take it ALL as a lump sum at retirement in place of receiving any additional pension.

4. If you do not choose the lump-sum option, a portion will be returned to you each year tax-free as part of your pension, and the amount and number of years will be based on the amount of your contributions and your average life-expectancy at the time of retirement.

In other words, if when you retire, you have an average life expectancy of 10 years, they will take your total contribution, divided by 10, and that amount will be included as part of your pension payments each year for the first 10 years of retirement. So part of your monthly pension check will be tax-free for the first 10 years. If you die prior to receiving the full reimbursement of your contributions, the unpaid balance will be paid as a lump-sum benefit to your beneficiaries.

If you live BEYOND your life expectancy, your pension will remain the same, but it will no longer have the tax-free portion from your contributions. This has very small implications for the FERS or CSRS Offset retiree, since the bulk of their contributions were paid to Social Security, and not into the retirement fund. But for the Civil Service retiree, this can have HUGE ramifications in the later stages of retirement. Look at this example:

Bill is a CSRS employee who retires at age 67 after 42 years with the government. His retirement contributions and interest total $112,000. At retirement, OPM determines his average life-expectancy to be 7 years. His monthly pension is 80% of his $64,000 high-three base salary, or $48,000/year. His contributions ($112,000) will be returned to him as part of his pension for the next seven years at $16,000/year. So Bill's pension will be $4,000/month, but because part of that is repayment of his contributions, he will owe taxes on less than $3,000 per month. Bill thinks this is GREAT... until he outlives his life expectancy. After age 74, his contributions are fully repaid, and he now owes taxes on the whole amount he receives. Because of taxes, his check will without warning be reduced by $300-500 per month.

Your repayment schedule will be set at the time you retire based on the current average life-expectancy tables, and your contributions.

CHAPTER EIGHT:

Maximizing Retirement Income

This chapter will answer some important questions about the two primary retirement systems: Civil Service Retirement System (CSRS), and Federal Employee Retirement System (FERS). With a few exceptions, CSRS employees are those hired prior to January 1, 1984, or those with at least 5 years of CSRS service who left and returned to work before January 1, 1988. FERS employees are those hired after January 1, 1984.

The CSRS pension grows by 2% each year up to 42 years of service, which, on a $52,000 annual salary, is about $80 in additional monthly retirement income for every year of additional work. The FERS employee pension will grow by 1% each year, adding about $40/month in retirement income.

In addition, the FERS employee who delays drawing Social Security until age 66 will generally add $300-400/month in retirement income. Working 2 or 3 extra years also gives time to add to TSP and other investment funds, which will increase future income. Working into your retirement years may not be your first choice, but sometimes it simply becomes a necessity for survival. No matter what your specific situation is, the closer we get to retirement, the more important it becomes to maximize the value of every dollar.

We've already suggested the best way to put money "IN" the TSP is by contributing the full amount the government will match. Take advantage of all the free money they'll give you. Getting the money "OUT" and putting it to good use should follow the same principle of high return and low risk.

During your separation and retirement process, Shared Services will offer you two available options for taking your funds out of the TSP:

1. First, you can CASH it out, and pay the total owed taxes on the whole amount in one year. If you have any sort of accumulation at all, this will put you into a higher tax bracket and further reduce any gains. Most employees know high taxes and a lump sum will not provide the life-income they need.

2. The second option they offer is to SELL your TSP. They don't call it that. They call it an annuity, but the reality of the second choice is to sell your accumulated TSP funds in exchange for a monthly income. The federal annuity will pay a lifetime income of approximately $600 each month for every $100,000 in your TSP.

To a retiring employee faced with a significant reduction in income, and compared to Option 1, the extra dollars from the annuity look pretty attractive and most employees choose Option

2. Without reading the fine print, this can be a very costly decision. In effect, you lose all rights to the principle. Also:

- There is no growth if/when the market recovers. Your payments are locked in with only cost-of-living increases.

- There is no death benefit. You may choose a reduced monthly payment and select a survivor option. However, there is no guarantee the total payout will match or exceed your beginning balance, and all payments stop with the death of the recipients.

- There is no inheritance to pass on to family members, and no final expense fund.

- There is no provision to access a larger portion of the money should funds be needed for nursing home care, terminal illness or other life events.

- The federal annuity essentially pays out interest in the form of monthly payments and keeps all the principle.

Don't be discouraged. There is a third option available. (We know, because they print the forms.) As with all 401k money, TSP funds can be withdrawn and "rolled-over" into qualified plans. There are hundreds of plans available and dozens of companies outside the government that would LOVE to help manage your money.

Sorting through them can be a nightmare, even for the expert, and it IS a job for an expert. It is well worth the effort to consult someone who specializes in this field. When it comes to understanding all the nuances and fine print of financial investing, you will do well to put your trust in someone who knows what they're doing. The expert would have a solid history and proven track record of consistent gains, even in the unstable market of the past few years.

At Federal Benefits Group, our investment philosophy with retirement funds is ZERO RISK. We have seen consistent returns with NO LOSSES win out over high risk year after year. We do not charge for consultations, nor are there any upfront, back-end or annual service fees. Our national research team stays up-to-date on every policy available in every state, and ensures our Benefit Specialists throughout the United States are educated, licensed and prepared to assist federal employees with the best available products.

For the past 12 years, the solutions we recommend have averaged consistent 8-10% gains, with no losses. In fact, they guarantee ZERO LOSS and zero risk on your investments. The rules vary state to state, but generally, our solutions have some very positive features that make them ideal for the retiring federal worker:

- Growth is tied to a market index, but the funds are not invested in the market.

- All funds are guaranteed. It can only grow. It has ZERO RISK of loss.

- You maintain access to 10% of your funds each year without penalty.

- You retain control and ownership of the principle.

- Access to additional portions of the principle is available without penalty in event of an extended nursing home stay or a terminal illness.

- All funds become immediately available to beneficiaries in event of death.

- In most states, policies are available that pay up-front bonuses – as much as 12%. Some pay additional 5-8% annual bonuses, as well as guaranteed lifetime income riders.

A Benefit Specialist can show you what is available in your state and help you determine what choices you have with your specific situation.

Final Recommendations

The federal benefits and retirement package has four common problems that employees often don't discover until it's too late to change:

1. Retirement income has a higher tax liability than they anticipated.

2. With FEGLI, employees pay higher-than market rates for life insurance, yet most are under-insured at their point of need.

3. Investment options in the TSP are low-return or high-risk, making it difficult to create enough retirement income.

4. Most federal employees will be forced into a lower standard of living and will be under-funded in retirement.

Our experience in working with thousands of federal employees teaches us that no one solution is right for every situation, and that in most cases we can only reduce, not eliminate, these four problems. The following *suggestions*, while general, when applied to specific situations have made the difference by hundreds of thousands of dollars for many federal employees.

We understand your benefit package, its strengths and weaknesses. We know how to help you get the most from your retirement partner (the US government) and show you the choices to allow you to take responsibility for your future.

Remember, ultimately it's all about YOU.

Minimize Tax Liability

1 Take full advantage of the government-matched funds to your TSP contributions.

2. Open a Roth IRA (if you qualify) and maximize your contributions to it: $5,000 per year up to age 50, and $6,000 for those 50 and older. This earns tax-free interest and the benefits are substantial!

3. Annuitize all TSP funds as quickly as possible – age 59½ or separation from federal service, whichever comes first. THESE PRODUCTS AND RULES CHANGE FREQUENTLY. Check our website for a Benefit Specialist near you who can give you the most current information for your specific situation.

Resolve Insurance Issues

1. Do an insurance analysis. Our Benefit Specialist can help.

2. Determine the amount of insurance needed, IF ANY.

3. Carry only as much insurance as you need, and only for as long as you need it.

4. Make certain you qualify for new insurance before canceling any existing insurance.

5. Don't overpay! Insurance rates vary. Our Benefit Specialists compare 14 companies.

6. Participate in investment or savings programs that create adequate and accessible funds to reduce or eliminate the need for insurance altogether.

Reduce Investment Risk

1. Grow your TSP through the matching funds and take advantage of guaranteed interest rates.

2. Open a Roth IRA with a guaranteed rate of interest and MAXIMIZE your annual contribution. In many cases, the underwriting insurance portion will decrease and will be less than the tax liability of those same dollars in a 401k plan.

3. At retirement or 59 ½ (whichever comes first), roll all available TSP funds into guaranteed growth annuities or life-income investments.

4. Compare before paying service charges or annual fees! The best programs available do not charge for using your money. In fact, many will pay you bonuses.

Increase Retirement Income

1. Invest at least 10% of every dollar earned. For employees earning $52,000 / year, that's $200 / paycheck.

2. If you're just starting to invest and you're over 30, invest 15%. ($300/paycheck.)

3. If you're over 40 and just getting started, you will want to invest 15-20%. ($300-400/paycheck.)

4. Your first dollars should go into the TSP to take advantage of the matching funds.

5. Your next dollars should be directed into a Roth IRA with guaranteed interest. MAXIMIZE that fund every year!

6. Additional funds should go toward debt reduction, equity or purchasing hard assets or real property.

7. DO NOT use your retirement for speculation, no matter how sure it looks, or making loans to friends or family, no matter how urgent the need.

The 7 Habits of Highly Ineffective TSP Investing

We've all heard of the 7 Habits of Highly Effective this or that, but in this final chapter we'd like to share with you a kind of "how NOT to do it approach" called **The 7 Habits of Highly Ineffective TSP Investing**. In other words, if you learn from the following 7 mistakes you will be well on your way to becoming Effective TSP Investors:

The 1st Habit of Highly Ineffective TSP Investing: *Not Contributing to TSP*

According to data provided by the Profit Sharing/401k council of America, about 17% of all people eligible to participate in 401k-like plans such as the TSP don't. Are people simply investing their money in other ways? There's not enough data to know for sure, but it's a safe bet that since retirement can seem so far off for any of us, it's easy to procrastinate.

We find out too late to do much about it; we haven't saved enough to nail down a secure retirement. What we often do is violate the key requirements of wealth accumulation:

1. Sufficient time for money to compound,

2. Adequate money doing the compounding, and

3. A sufficient level earnings on those dollars over time.

Time is the most important factor. For FERS employees all the money contributed to their accounts vests immediately with the exception of the first 1% automatic agency contribution (taking three employment yrs. to vest). This means the FERS employee earns 100% on his/her investment at the 5% contribution level.

Where else can one invest like this?

The 2nd Habit of Highly Ineffective TSP Investing: *Failing to Max-out TSP Contributions*

Many employees fail to maximize their allowable TSP contribution – and their rationalizations are many and varied. Some employees say (especially FERS workers) that they'll only contribute to get the government's 5% match and they will invest the rest in Roth IRA's, etc. This often fails because of bad spending behavior.

Once a contribution is made to the TSP the amount is "out of sight, out of mind" and the money is seldom missed. Programs outside of the TSP require more discipline to make installment payments because they lack similar automatic contribution mechanisms. (In the case of Roth IRAs, which allow withdrawal with no further taxes or penalties, it's too easy to withdraw those invested dollars to cover relatively minor emergencies, a new car and so on.)

The most common rationalization is "I can't afford it because..." Nearly anyone who has the desire to can afford to contribute the maximum to the TSP. It simply becomes a matter of spending priorities. The real statement should be: "I don't want to set aside that much to the TSP because I want to do other things with my money." If you accept this reasoning, you're really saying that you are willing to postpone retirement to buy something you want now!

Maximum contributions are imperative for FERS workers unless they are independently wealthy or have a second source of income.

When the government instituted FERS, it was following corporate America in changing retirement systems from defined benefit systems (CSRS) to defined contribution systems (FERS). The distinction meant that FERS employees would have to depend more heavily upon their TSP investments than CSRS employees would. (However, although CSRS employees, who receive no matching government contributions to the TSP, it's still a good idea to contribute the maximum to the TSP.)

The 3rd Habit of Highly Ineffective TSP Investing: *Not Keeping Beneficiary Designations Current*

It seems like a small detail, but it can have enormous negative consequences if you get careless. A completed and witnessed designation of beneficiary form, with rare exception, could override any designation of beneficiary that you have stated in your will. It is very important for you to periodically review your records to make sure you have completed a designation of beneficiary form, and to determine whether or not you need to cancel or change your designation.

This is very important in the case of divorce, legal separation, death of a family member, etc. If you already have retired, you might want to complete a new designation of beneficiary form (TSP-3) and forward to the TSP Service Office in New Orleans. A new form automatically supersedes any prior form that you may have completed. If you do not have a completed beneficiary form, the proceeds will be paid according to the government's "order of preference," and this may not be what you want.

Why let the government disperse your proceeds?

The 4th Habit of Highly Ineffective TSP Investing: *Paying Off Mortgages with TSP Funds*

We all would like to retire debt free. Having no mortgage payment is tempting. You could take a lump sum withdrawal from the TSP to pay off the house. This could be a big financial mistake that could cost you tens of thousands of dollars. Assuming a $50,000 dollar mortgage at retirement and a federal pension of $35,000, the adjusted gross income of this taxpayer is at least $85,000 dollars if the mortgage is paid off using the TSP (withdrawals from the TSP are taxable income by the IRS).

The difference in taxable income rates in this example is 10 percentage points (15% at $35,000 of income vs. 25% at $85,000 of income) costing this taxpayer an additional $12,500 in tax that must be paid from somewhere. The error is compounded as the amount needed to pay off the mortgage grows. While the charm of no mortgage payment is strong, the cost of paying it off with the TSP could be extremely high.

The 5th Habit of Highly Ineffective TSP Investing:
Neglecting to Understand Your TSP Withdrawal Options

Very few government workers seem to understand how the different TSP withdrawal options work. It's important to know your options but even more critical when you retire and have to make a choice. Few pick the Designated Payment or Lifetime Annuity options because of preconceived ideas as to the value of doing so or because they simply do not understand them. We suggest that they are worthy of consideration in many (not all) circumstances where one needs an "income bridge" for a certain period or where living to a ripe old age runs in the family. Your money needs to be guaranteed to last a long time. There are ways to extend guaranteed income using TSP options if you understand them.

Surprisingly, one choice often overlooked by many federal employees is the annuity option. The risk of outliving one's money is growing every day. Life expectancies in the US are getting longer as medical technologies advance. When Social Security was born, mortality in the US was an average 63 years.

Today that average lifespan is 78 – and rising. Running out of money in retirement is a real possibility. The only choice available in the TSP that guarantees lifetime income is the annuity option. While not generally a good idea for all of one's liquid assets, it can help in your overall income strategy. When examining the need for guaranteed income for expenses such as health care, food, clothing, shelter, etc., annuitizing a portion of the TSP can make good sense. So, make sure you give it more than a cursory look.

The 6th Habit of Highly Ineffective TSP Investing: *Being Too Financially Conservative — Or Aggressive*

Studies show that the federal government employee who is too conservative with TSP fund allocations faces the real possibility of running out of money before death. For example, if you could earn 6% in the G fund (substantially higher than today's rates), investing $100,000, take out the interest and buy a 3.5% COLA on the income to counteract inflation, you'd run out of TSP money in 21 years. That means if you retired at 55 you'd be without TSP income at age 76. Another way of looking at it is that if you lived to age 85, you may have had to stay in government until age 64 to bank enough TSP money to cover those extra years of income.

Meanwhile, being overly aggressive with one's TSP allocations can be just as bad as being too timid. By chasing returns, believing against all evidence to the contrary that markets only go up, it's easy to see why so many retirees of the late 1990's invested themselves back into employment! While it is necessary to take some equity risk to give your portfolio a chance to outdo inflation, it's also prudent to understand when the markets are overvalued.

The 7th Habit of Highly Ineffective TSP Investing: *Trying to Time the Market*

There are a number of companies/services claiming to have success in timing TSP investment (making numerous switches among various funds). Their track records are far from stellar! Fear, greed and emotional conditions seem to drive the markets that are impossible to accurately measure. With terrorism factoring into the markets today, it's even more uncertain what will happen tomorrow. The only thing we know for sure about the future is that it's always uncertain.

If successful market timing is virtually not possible, then what course of action makes sense for your TSP investments? Understanding that risk is not only capital risk, but longevity risk, will help you allocate your TSP dollars. It makes sense to rebalance your account, especially if you have had or expect to have significant changes in your life. This results in a mix that is suitable for age, the need for withdrawal, and the ability to sleep at night.

Glossary of Terms

1035 exchange

Section 1035 sets out provisions for the exchange of similar (insurance related) assets without any tax consequence upon the conversion. If the exchange qualifies for like-kind exchange consideration, income taxes are deferred until the new property or asset is sold. The 1035 exchange provisions are only available for a limited type of asset which includes cash value life insurance policies and annuity contracts.

401(k) plan

A 401(k) plan is a tax-deferred defined contribution retirement plan that gives eligible employees the opportunity to defer a portion of their current compensation into the plan. Amounts that are deferred are excluded from the participant's gross income for the year of the deferral. The plan may provide for employer matching contributions and discretionary profit-sharing contributions.

403(b) plan

Tax deferred annuity retirement plan available to employees of public schools and colleges, and certain non-profit hospitals, charitable, religious, scientific and educational organizations.

457 plan

Non-qualified deferred compensation plans available to employees of state and local governments and tax-exempt organizations.

A

Accelerated death benefits (adb's)

Some life insurance policies make a portion of the death benefit available prior to the death of the insured. Such benefits are usually available only due to terminal illness or for long-term care situations.

Accidental death benefit

An accidental death benefit is a rider added to an insurance policy which provides that an additional death benefit will be paid in the event death is caused by an accident. This rider is often called "double indemnity."

Account balance

Account balance, also called your accrued benefit, is the amount your 401(k) account is worth on a date that it's valued. For example, if the value of your account on December 31 is $250,000, that's your account balance. Each time your account is valued, it is likely to have a new balance.

Adjustable rate mortgage (arm)

An adjustable Rate Mortgage offers an initial interest rate that is usually lower than a fixed rate, but that adjusts periodically according to market conditions and financial indices. The rate may go up and/or down, depending on economic conditions. To limit the borrower's risk, the ARM will almost always have a maximum interest rate allowed, called a "rate cap."

After-tax investments

After-tax investments you make with income on which you have already paid income tax.

Amortization

The amortization of a debt is its systematic repayment through installments of principal and interest. An amortization schedule is a periodic table illustrating payments, principal, interest, and outstanding balance.

Annual percentage rate (apr)

The Annual Percentage Rate is the cost of credit expressed as a yearly rate. The APR is a means of comparing loans offered by various lenders on equal terms, taking into account interest rates, points, and other finance charges. The federal Truth-in-Lending Act requires disclosure of the APR.

Annuitant

An individual who receives payments from an annuity. The person whose life the annuity payments are measured on or determined by.

Annuity

A contract between an insurance company and an individual which generally guarantees lifetime income to the individual or whose life the contract is based in return for either a lump sum or periodic payment to the insurance company. Interest earned inside an annuity is income tax-deferred until it is paid out or withdrawn.

Asset allocation

Asset allocation is a strategy for offsetting systematic risk by investing specific percentages of your investment principal in different asset classes. For example, you might put 60% of your 401(k) portfolio in equity investments, 30% in fixed income investments, and 10% in cash equivalents. You use different asset allocation models and include different asset classes in your portfolio based on your investment objectives, your risk tolerance, and your timeframe.

B

Basis points

Basis points is a term used by investment professionals to describe yields of bonds. One basis point equals one 100th of 1%, or .01%. A bond yield increase from 10.0% to 10.1% represents an increase of 10 basis points.

Bear market

A prolonged decline in overall stock prices occurring over a period of months or even years.

Benchmark

Benchmark is a standard against which some variable is measured. A market index or average whose gains and losses reflect the changing direction of the market segment it tracks – such as large company stocks or corporate bonds – may serve as a benchmark for individual securities included in the index and mutual funds investing in those securities.

Beneficiary

The person who is designated to receive the benefits of a contract.

Beta

A statistically generated number that is used to measure the volatility of a security or mutual fund in comparison to the market as a whole.

Bid price

The price that a buyer is willing to pay for a security or commodity.

Blue-chip stocks

The equity issues of financially stable, well-established companies that usually have a history of being able to pay dividends in bear and bull markets.

Bond

A certificate of indebtedness issued by a government entity or a corporation, which pays a fixed cash coupon at regular intervals. The coupon payment is normally a fixed percentage of the initial investment. The face value of the bond is repaid to the investor upon maturity.

Bonding requirement

The individual(s) that are appointed to run the day-to-day operations of a qualified plan, as well as the trustee(s) and investment manager(s) must be bonded. The bond is required to provide protection to the plan against loss due to fraud, theft, forgery or dishonesty.

Brokerage window

Brokerage window is a designated brokerage account offered as an investment option in a 401(k) plan. Through a window, a plan participant is able to buy and sell individual securities and other investments. While the percentage of plans offering brokerage windows is increasing, opinion is divided on the wisdom of giving participants so wide a choice.

Bull market

A prolonged increase in overall stock prices usually occurring over a period of months or even years.

C

Capital gains tax

Capital gains tax may be due when you sell taxable investments for more than you paid to buy them. The tax on long-term gains, which applies to the sale of investments you've owned more than a year, is calculated at a maximum rate of 15% and may be as low as 5%.

Capital preservation

Capital preservation is an investment strategy designed to protect the assets you have. In most cases, you choose insured investments or other products that pose little or no risk to the principal. However, in using this strategy you do expose yourself to inflation risk since you're likely to realize only a marginal increase in the value of your portfolio.

Cash value

Permanent life insurance policies provide both a death benefit and an investment component called a cash value. The cash value earns interest and often appreciates. The policyholder may accumulate significant cash value over the years and, in some circumstances, "borrow" the appreciated funds without paying taxes on the borrowed gains. As long as the policy stays in force the borrowed funds do not need to be repaid, but interest may be charged to your cash value account.

Certificate of deposit (cd)

A Certificate of Deposit is a low risk, often federally guaranteed investment offered by banks. A CD pays interest to investors for as long as five years. The interest rate on a CD is fixed for the duration of the CD term.

Charitable remainder trust (crt)

The Charitable Remainder Trust is an irrevocable trust with both charitable and non-charitable beneficiaries. The donor transfers highly appreciated assets into the trust and retains an income interest. Upon expiration of the income interest, the remainder in the trust passes to a qualified charity of the donor's choice. If properly structured, the CRT permits the donor to receive income, estate, and/or gift tax advantages. These advantages often provide for a much greater income stream to the income beneficiary than would be available outside the trust.

Co-borrower

A co-borrower is individually or jointly obligated to repay a loan entered into with a third party. The co-borrower may or may not share in ownership of loan collateral.

Codicil

An instrument in writing executed by a testator for adding to, altering, explaining or confirming a will previously made by the testator; executed with the same formalities as a will; and having the effect of bringing the date of the will forward to the date of codicil.

Collateral

Assets pledged as security for a loan. If the borrower defaults on payment, the lender may dispose of the property pledged as security to raise money to repay the loan.

Commission

The fee a broker or insurance agent collects for administering a trade or policy.

Commodity

A commodity is a physical substance such as a food or a metal which investors buy or sell on a commodities exchange, usually via futures contracts.

Common stock

A security that represents ownership in a corporation.

Compounding

The computation of interest paid using the principal plus the previously earned interest.

Conduit IRA

An individual who rolled over a total distribution from a qualified plan into an IRA can later roll over those assets into a new employer's plan. In this case the IRA has been used as a holding account (a conduit).

Conforming loan

A mortgage loan that conforms to Federal National Mortgage Association (FNMA) or Federal Home Loan Mortgage Corporation (FHLMC) guidelines. Currently, conforming first mortgages are under $275,000 ($413,000 in Alaska and Hawaii).

Consumer debt

Debt incurred for consumable or depreciating non-investment assets. Items include credit card debt, store-financed consumer purchases, car loans, and family loans that will be repaid.

Conventional mortgage

A conventional mortgage is not insured, guaranteed or funded by the Veterans Administration, the Federal Housing Administration, or Rural Economic Community Development.

Convertible term insurance

Term life insurance that can be converted to a permanent or whole life policy without evidence of insurability, subject to time limitations.

Credit bureau repositories

A credit bureau repository is an organization that compiles credit history information directly from lenders and creditors into credit summaries and reports. These reports are made available to lenders and creditors to assist them in gauging an individual's credit worthiness.

Critical illness insurance

Insurance protection designed to provide a lump-sum payment equal to the full value of the policy or a percentage of the policy depending upon the product design, to the insured/policy owner upon the diagnosis of a covered critical illness. Typical illnesses covered include heart attack, stroke, cancer, paralysis, renal failure and Alzheimer's disease. Many policies offer a partial payment for certain medical procedures such as coronary bypass surgery or angioplasty. Some policies offer a return of all premiums in the event of death of the insured, others pay the full benefit upon the insured's death.

Custodian

A financial institution, usually a bank or trust company, that holds a person or company's cash and or securities in safekeeping.

D

Debit cards

Debit cards allow the cost of a purchase to be automatically deducted from the customer's bank account and credited to the merchant.

Debt markets

The fixed income sector of the capital markets devoted to trading debt securities issued by corporations and governments.

Debt to income ratio

The ratio of a person's total monthly debt obligations compared to their total monthly resources is called their debt to income ratio. This ratio is used to evaluate a borrower's capacity to repay debts.

Decedent

The term decedent refers to a person who has died.

Decreasing term

A term life insurance featuring a decreasing death benefit. Decreasing term is well suited to provide for an obligation that decreases over the years such as a mortgage.

Deed of trust

A document used to convey title (ownership) to a property used as collateral for a loan to a trustee pending the repayment of the loan. The equivalent of a mortgage.

Deferral

A form of tax sheltering in which all earnings are allowed to compound tax-free until they are withdrawn at a future date. Placing funds in a qualified plan, for example, triggers deductions (not all qualified plans provide for tax deductions; contributions may, however, be excluded from gross income, i.e. 401(k) plans) for the current tax year and postpones capital gains or other income taxes until the funds are withdrawn from the plan.

Deferred compensation

Income withheld by an employer and paid at some future time, usually upon retirement or termination of employment.

Defined benefit plan

A defined benefit plan pays participants a specific retirement benefit that is promised (defined) in the plan document. Under a defined benefit plan benefits must be definitely determinable. For example, a plan that entitles a participant to a monthly pension benefit for life equal to 30 percent of monthly compensation is a defined benefit plan.

Defined contribution plan

In a defined contribution plan, contributions are allocated to individual accounts according to a pre-determined contribution allocation. This type of plan does not promise any specific dollar benefit to a participant at retirement. Benefits received are based on amounts contributed, investment performance and vesting. The most common type of defined contribution plan is the 401(k) profit-sharing plan.

Deflation

A period in which the general price level of goods and services is declining.

Depreciation

Charges made against earnings to write off the cost of a fixed asset over its estimated useful life. Depreciation does not represent a cash outlay. It is a bookkeeping entry representing the decline in value of an asset over time.

Direct deposit

A means of authorizing payment made by governments or companies to be deposited directly into a recipient's account. Used mainly for the deposit of salary, pension and interest checks.

Disability insurance

Insurance designed to replace a percentage of earned income if accident or illness prevents the beneficiary from pursuing his or her livelihood.

Disposable income

After-tax income available for spending, saving or investing.

Diversification

Spreading investment risk among a number of different securities, properties, companies, industries or geographical locations. Diversification does not assure against market loss.

Dividend reinvestment plan (drip)

An investment plan that allows shareholders to receive stock in lieu of cash dividends.

Dividends

A distribution of the earnings of a company to it's shareholders. Dividends are "declared" by the company based on profitability and can change from time to time. There is a direct relationship between dividends paid and share value growth. The most aggressive growth companies do not pay a dividend, and the highest dividend paying companies may not experience dramatic growth.

Dollar cost averaging

Buying a mutual fund or securities using a consistent dollar amount of money each month (or other period). More securities will be bought when prices are low, resulting in lowering the average cost per share. Dollar cost averaging neither guarantees a profit nor eliminates the risk of losses in declining markets and you should consider your ability to continue investing through periods of market volatility and/or low prices.

E

Economic cycle

Economic events are often felt to repeat a regular pattern over a period of anywhere from two to eight years. This pattern of events ends to be slightly different each time, but usually has a large number of similarities to previous cycles.

Effective tax rate

The percentage of total income paid in federal and state income taxes.

Efficient market

The market in which all the available information has been analyzed and is reflected in the current stock price.

Employee stock ownership plans (esops)

An ESOP plan allows employees to purchase stock, usually at a discount, that they can hold or sell. ESOPs offer a tax advantage for both employer and employee. The employer earns a tax deduction for contributions of stock or cash used to purchase stock for the employee. The employee pays no tax on these contributions until they are distributed.

Estate

A decedent's estate is equal to the total value of their assets as of the date of death. The estate includes all funds, personal effects, interest in business enterprises, titles to property, real estate, stocks, bonds and notes receivable.

Estate planning

The orderly arrangement of one's financial affairs to maximize the value transferred at death to the people and institutions favored by the deceased, with minimum loss of value because of taxes and forced liquidation of assets.

Excess distributions

An individual may have to pay a 15% tax on distributions received from qualified plans in excess of $150,000 during a single year. The tax, however, does not apply to distributions due to death, distributions that are rolled over, and distributions of after-tax contributions.

Executor

The person named in a will to manage the estate of the deceased according to the terms of the will.

F

Face amount

The face amount stated in a life insurance policy is the amount that will be paid upon death, or policy maturity. The face amount of a permanent insurance policy may change with time as the cash value in the policy increases.

Family trust

An inter vivos trust established with family members as beneficiaries.

Federal housing administration (fha)

The Federal Housing Administration (FHA) is a government agency that sets standards for underwriting residential mortgage loans made by private lenders and insures such transactions.

Federal national mortgage association (fnma or fannie mae).

FNMA is a private corporation that acts as a secondary market investor in buying and selling mortgage loans.

Fiduciary

An individual or institution occupying a position of trust. An executor, administrator or trustee.

Financial planner

A person who helps you plan and carry out your financial future.

Fixed investment

Any investment paying a fixed interest rate such as a money market account, a certificate of deposit, a bond, a note, or a preferred stock. A fixed investment is the opposite of a variable investment.

Fixed rate mortgage

With a fixed rate mortgage, your interest rate will remain the same for the entire term of the loan. Although the rate will begin slightly higher than a comparable adjustable rate mortgage (ARM), the interest rate you pay can never go up for as long as you have the mortgage.

Full retirement age

Full retirement age is the age at which you qualify to collect your full Social Security benefit. It is scheduled to increase form 65 to 67 in two-month increments. For example, people born in 1942 must be 65 and 10 months to reach full retirement age.

Fund of funds

See Life cycle fund definition.

G

Group insurance

A form of insurance designed to insure classes of persons rather than specific individuals.

Growth stock

The common equity of a company that consistently grows significantly faster than the economy.

Guaranteed investment certificate (gic)

A type of debt security sold to individuals by banks and trust companies. They usually cannot be cashed before the specified redemption date, and pay interest at a fixed rate.

Guaranteed lifetime income

Guaranteed lifetime income is money paid from a pension or an annuity over your lifetime, or the combined lifetimes of you and your surviving beneficiary.

Guarantor

A third party who agrees to repay any outstanding balance on a loan if you fail to do so. A guarantor is responsible for the debt only if the principal debtor defaults on the loan.

Guardian

A person or persons named to care for minor children until they reach the age of majority. A will is the best way to ensure that the person or persons whom you wish to have care for your minor children are legally empowered to do so in the event of your death.

H

Home equity line of credit (heloc)

A home equity line of credit allows a homeowner to borrow against the equity in their home with specific limits and terms. This is an open end loan which allows the borrower to borrow and repay funds as needed.

Home equity loan

A home equity loan is a collateralized mortgage, usually in a subordinate position, entered into by the property owner under specific terms of repayment.

I

Illustration

A life insurance illustration, or ledger, is a reference tool used to illustrate how a given life insurance policy underwritten by a specific insurer is expected to perform over a period of years. The insurance illustration assumes that conditions remain unchanged over the period of time that the policy is held.

Income averaging

Income averaging allows individuals who were age 50 before January 1, 1986 to pay tax on a lump sum distribution as though it had been received over a five or ten year period, rather than all at once. By using income averaging individuals may be able to pay income tax at a more favorable rate.

Individual retirement account (ira)

An Individual Retirement Account (IRA) is a personal savings plan that offers tax advantages to those who set aside money for retirement. Depending on the individual's circumstances, contributions to the IRA may be deductible in whole or in part. Generally, amounts in an IRA, including earnings and gains, are not taxed until distributed to the individual.

Inflation

A term used to describe the economic environment of rising prices and declining purchasing power.

In-force policy

An in-force life insurance policy is simply a valid policy. Generally speaking, a life insurance policy will remain in-force as long as sufficient premiums are paid, and for approximately 31 days thereafter. (See Grace Period.)

Insurability

Insurability refers to the assessment of the applicant's health and is used to gauge the level of risk the insurer would potentially take by underwriting a policy, and therefore the premium it must charge.

insured

A life insurance policy covers the life of one or more insured individuals.

Interest rate

The simple interest rate attached to the terms of a mortgage or other loan. This rate is applied to the outstanding principal owed in determining the portion of a payment attributable to interest and to principal in any given payment.

Interest rate risk

Is the uncertainty in the direction of interest rates. Changes in interest rates could lead to capital loss, or a yield less than that available to other investors, Putting at risk the earnings capacity of capital.

Intestate

A term describing the legal status of a person who dies without a will.

Investment banker

A firm that engages in the origination, underwriting, and distribution of new issues.

Investment company

A corporation or trust whose primary purpose is to invest the funds of its shareholders.

Investment considerations

Choosing which investments are right for you will depend on a number of factors, including; your primary objectives, your time horizon and your risk tolerance.

Investment portfolio

A term used to describe your total investment holdings.

Investment risk

The chance that the actual returns realized on an investment will differ from the expected return.

Investment strategy

The method used to select which assets to include in a portfolio and to decide when to buy and when to sell those assets.

IRA (individual retirement account)

An Individual Retirement Account (IRA) is a personal savings plan that offers tax advantages to those who set aside money for retirement. Depending on the individual's circumstances, contributions to the IRA may be deductible in whole or in part. Generally, amounts in an IRA, including earnings and gains, are not taxed until distributed to the individual.

IRA rollover

An individual may withdraw, tax-free, all or part of the assets from one IRA, and reinvest them within 60 days in another IRA. A rollover of this type can occur only once in any one-year period. The one-year rule applies separately to each IRA the individual owns. An individual must roll over into another IRA the same property he/she received from the old IRA.

J

Jumbo loan

A loan that is larger than the limits set for conventional loans by the Federal National Mortgage Association (FNMA) or Federal Home Loan Mortgage Corportation (FHLMC). This limit is currently set at $300,700.

Junk bonds

A bond that pays an unusually higher rate of return to compensate for a low credit rating.

K

Keogh

A Keogh is a tax deferred retirement plan for self-employed individuals and employees of unincorporated businesses. A Keogh plan is similar to an IRA but with significantly higher contribution limits.

L

Lien

A lien represents a claim against a property or asset for the payment of a debt. Examples include a mortgage, a tax lien, a court judgment, etc.

Life cycle fund

Life cycle fund, sometimes called a fund of funds, is a package of individual mutual funds that a fund company puts together to help investors meet their objectives without having to select a portfolio of funds on their own. Some companies offer a set of three to five separate life cycle funds, each with a different level of risk and potential for return. You can choose from among them the specific package that suits your investment style or that's appropriate for reaching your goals within the timeframe you have allowed.

Life expectancy

Life expectancy represents the average future time an individual can expect to live. Life expectancies have been increasing steadily over the past century and may continue to increase in the future. As people are living longer the cost of retirement is increasing.

Life insurance

A contract between you and a life insurance company that specifies that the insurer will provide either a stated sum or a periodic income to your designated beneficiaries upon your death.

Life settlement

Occurs when a person who does not have a terminal or chronic illness sells his/her life insurance policy to a third party for an amount that is less than the full amount of the death benefit. The buyer becomes the new owner and/or beneficiary of the life insurance policy, pays all future premiums, and collects the entire death benefit when the the insured dies. Some states regulate the purchase as a security while others may regulate it as insurance.

Liquidity

Liquidity is the measure of your ability to immediately turn assets into cash without penalty or risk of loss. Examples include a savings account, money market account, checking account, etc.

Living wills

If you become incapacitated this document will preserve your wishes and act as your voice in medical decisions, if you are unable to speak for yourself as a result of medical reasons.

Loan-to-value ratio

A loan-to-value ratio represents the relationship between all outstanding and proposed loans on a property and the appraised value of the property. For example, an $80,000 loan on a $100,000 property would represent an 80% loan-to-value ratio. This ratio assists a lender in determining the risk associated with the loan. The higher this ratio, the riskier the loan.

Long position

A long position in an investment indicates a current ownership in that investment which would increase in value as the underlying asset(s) increase in value, opposite of a short position.

M

Matching contribution

Matching contribution is money or company stock your employer adds to your 401(k) account, usually figured as a percentage of the amount you contribute. Employers are not required to match contributions, but may do so if they wish. Employers must also choose a vesting schedule that conforms to federal guidelines to determine how long you must be on the job to be entitled to transfer or withdraw the matching contributions.

Medical power of attorney

This special power of attorney document allows you to designate another person to make medical decisions on your behalf.

Minimum distributions

An individual must start receiving distributions from a qualified plan by April 1st of the year following the year in which he/she reaches age 70. Subsequent distributions must occur by each December 31st. The minimum distributions can be based on the life expectancy of the individual or the joint life expectancy of the individual and beneficiary.

Mortality

Mortality is the risk of death of a given person based on factors such as age, health, gender, and lifestyle.

Mortgage

A legal instrument providing a loan to the mortgagee to be used to purchase a real property in exchange for a lien against the property.

Mortgage broker

A mortgage broker acts as an intermediary between a borrower and a lender. A broker's expertise is to assist the borrower in identifying mortgage lenders and products that they might not identify otherwise.

Mortgage insurance (mi)

Mortgage insurance protects the lender against the default of higher risk loans. Most lenders require mortgage insurance on loans where the loan-to-value ratio is higher than 80% (less than 20% equity).

Municipal bonds

A bond offered by a state, county, city or other political entity (such as a school district) to raise public funds for special projects. The interest received from municipal bonds is often exempt from certain income taxes.

Mutual funds

A mutual fund is a pooling of investor (shareholder) assets, which is professionally managed by an investment company for the benefit of the fund's shareholders. Each fund has specific investment objectives and associated risk. Mutual funds offer shareholders the advantage of diversification and professional management in exchange for a management fee.

N

Net asset value

The value of all the holdings of a mutual fund, less the fund's liabilities (also describes the price at which fund shares are redeemed).

Net worth

Your net worth is the difference between your total assets and total liabilities.

Non-conforming loan

A loan that does not conform to Federal National Mortgage Association (FNMA) or Federal Home Loan Mortgage Corporation (FHLMC) guidelines. Such loans include jumbo loan, sub-prime loans and high risk loans. Also known as the type of loans that caused the mortgage crisis!

Note

A note is a legal document that acknowledges a debt and the terms and conditions agreed upon by the borrower.

O

Open-end fund

An open-end mutual fund continuously issues and redeems units, so the number of units outstanding varies from day to day. Most mutual funds are open-end funds. The opposite of closed-end fund.

Origination fee

The origination fee on a mortgage is usually the amount charged by the lender for originating the loan. Origination fees vary by lender and are expressed in points where one point is equal to 1% of the original loan balance.

Over-the-counter (otc) market

Market created by dealer trading as opposed to the auction market, which prevails on most major exchanges.

P

Paper gain (loss)

Unrealized capital gain (loss) on securities held in portfolio, based on a comparison of current market price to original cost.

Payroll deduction

Payments made on your behalf by your employer. They are automatically deducted from your pay check.

Points

Points are charges added to a mortgage loan by the lender and are based on the loan amount. One point is equal to 1% of the original loan balance.

Policy

A contractual arrangement between the insurer and the insured describing the terms and conditions of the life insurance contract.

Policy loan

The policy owner can borrow from the cash value component of many permanent insurance policies for virtually any purpose. Any policy loans that are outstanding at the time of death of the insured will be deducted from the benefit paid to the beneficiary.

Power of attorney

A legal document authorizing one person to act on behalf of another.

Premium

The payment that the owner of a life insurance policy makes to the insurer. In exchange for the premium payment, the insurer assumes the financial risk (as defined by the insurance policy) associated with the death of the insured.

Present value

The current worth of a future payment, or stream of payments, discounted at a given interest rate over a given period of time.

Pretax investments

Pretax investments are made with employment earnings subtracted from your pay before income tax is calculated and withheld. These investments, which are not reported as current income, go into a tax-deferred account. Income tax, calculated at your regular tax rate, is due on these investments and their earnings when you withdraw from that account.

Principal

The principal amount of a loan or mortgage is the outstanding balance, excluding interest.

Private mortgage insurance

Private mortgage insurance protects the lender against the default of higher risk loans. Most lenders require private mortgage insurance on loans where the loan-to-value ratio is higher than 80% (less than 20% equity).

Probate

The process used to make an orderly distribution and transfer of property from the deceased to a group of beneficiaries. The probate process is characterized by court supervision of property transfer, filing of claims against the estate by creditors and publication of a last will and testament.

Profit sharing plan

A Profit-Sharing Plan is the most flexible and simplest of the defined contribution plans. It permits discretionary annual contributions that are generally allocated on the basis of compensation. The employer will determine the amount to be contributed each year depending on the cash-flow of the company. The deduction for contributions to a Profit-Sharing Plan cannot be more than 15% of the compensation paid to the employees participating in the plan. Annual employer contributions to the account of a participant cannot exceed the smaller of $30,000 or 25 percent of a participant's compensation.

Prohibited ira transactions

Generally, a prohibited transaction is any improper (self-dealing) use of the IRA by the account owner. Some examples include borrowing money from an IRA, using an IRA to secure a loan and selling property to an IRA.

Prospectus

A detailed statement prepared by an issuer and filed with the SEC prior to the sale of a new issue. The prospectus gives detailed information on the issue and on the issuer's condition and prospects.

Q

Qualified retirement plan

A qualified retirement plan is a retirement plan that meets certain specified tax rules contained primarily in section 401(a) of the Internal Revenue Code. These rules are called "plan qualification rules." If the rules are satisfied the plan's trust is exempt from taxes.

R

Refinance

To refinance one's mortgage is to retire the existing mortgage using the proceeds of a new mortgage and using the same property as collateral. This is usually done to secure a lower interest rate mortgage or to access equity from the property.

Registered representative

A registered representative is licensed with the NASD (National Association of Securities Dealers), through association with an NASD member broker/dealer, to act as an account representative for clients and collect commission income.

Revolving debt

A debt or liability that does not have a fixed principal balance or payment. Examples include credit cards, home equity lines of credit, etc.

Rider

A life insurance rider is an amendment to the standard policy that expands or restricts the policy's benefits. Common riders include a disability waiver of premium rider and a children's life coverage rider.

Rule of 72

A way to determine the effect of compound interest. Divide 72 by the expected return on your investment. If your expected return is 8%, assuming that all interest is reinvested, you will double your money in 9 years.

S

Salary reduction simplified employee pension (sarsep)

A SARSEP is a simplified alternative to a 401(k) plan. It is a SEP that includes a salary reduction arrangement. Under this special arrangement, eligible employees can elect to have the employer contribute part of their before-tax pay to their IRA. This amount is called an "elective deferral."

SEC

The main regulatory body regulating the securities industry is called the Securities and Exchange Commission.

Securities

Stocks and bonds are traditionally referred to as securities. More specifically, stocks are often referred to as "equities" and bonds as "debt instruments."

Securities and Exchange Commission

The main regulatory body regulating the securities industry is called the Securities and Exchange Commission.

Simplified employee pension (sep)

A SEP provides employers with a "simplified" alternative to a qualified profit-sharing plan. Basically, a SEP is a written arrangement that allows an employer to make contributions towards his or her own and employees' retirement, without becoming involved in a more complex retirement plan. Under a SEP, IRAs are set up for each eligible employee. SEP contributions are made to IRAs of the participants in the plan. The employer has no control over the employee's IRA once the money is contributed.

Small cap

A small cap stock is one issued by a company with less than $1.7 billion in market capitalization.

Smart card

A card with an embedded computer chip which stores more information, performs more functions and is more secure than a credit card or debit card.

Spousal IRA

An individual can set up and contribute to an IRA for his/her spouse. This is called a "Spousal IRA" and can be established if certain requirements are met. In the case of a spousal IRA, the individual and spouse must have separate IRAs. A jointly owned IRA is not permitted.

Stock

Stock certificates represent an ownership position in a corporation. Stockholders are often entitled to dividends, voting rights, and financial participation in company growth.

Stock dividends

The investor's share of the income earned by the company issuing the stock.

Stock exchange

A market for trading of equities, a public market for the buying and selling of public stocks.

Surrender value

When a policy owner surrenders his/her permanent life insurance policy to the insurance company, he or she will receive the surrender value of that policy in return. The surrender value is the cash value of the policy plus any dividend accumulations, plus the cash value of any paid-up additions minus any policy loans, interest, and applicable surrender charges.

Systematic withdrawal

Systematic withdrawal is a plan you establish to receive income from a managed account, mutual fund, or variable annuity on a regular basis over a period of years. Systematic withdrawals are flexible, so you can change the amount if you wish. But you aren't guaranteed lifetime income.

T

Tax credit

An income tax credit directly reduces the amount of income tax paid by offsetting other income tax liabilities.

Tax deduction

A reduction of total income before the amount of income tax payable is calculated.

Tax-deferred

The term tax deferred refers to the deferral of income taxes on interest earnings until the interest is withdrawn from the investment. Some vehicles or products that enjoy this special tax treatment include permanent life insurance, annuities, and any investment held in IRA's.

Technical analysis

Technical analysis is a technique of estimating a stock's future value strictly by examining its prices and volume of trading over time. Technical analysis is the opposite of fundamental analysis.

Term insurance

Term insurance is life insurance coverage that pays a death benefit only if the insured dies within a specified period of time. Term policies do not have a cash value component and must be renewed periodically as dictated by the insurance contract.

Testamentary trust

A trust created under the terms of a will and that takes effect upon the death of the testator.

Ticker symbol

A ticker symbol is a combination of letters that identifies a stock-exchange security.

Title

A legal document establishing property ownership.

Total disability

In order to make a disability claim a person must meet the definition of disability set forth in the insurance contract. There are two general definitions of disability used in today's contracts. The first definition is that the insured is unable to perform all of the substantial and material duties of his/her own occupation. The second, and more restrictive, definition is that the insured is unable to perform any occupation for which he/she is reasonably suited by education, training, or experience.

Treasury bill

Treasury bills, often referred to as T-bills, are short-term securities (maturities of less than one year) offered and guaranteed by the federal government. They are issued at a discount and pay their full face value at maturity.

Treasury bond

Treasury bonds are issued with maturities of more than 10 years and are offered and guaranteed by the U.S. Government. They are issued at a discount and pay their full face value at maturity.

Treasury note

Treasury notes are issued with maturities between one and 10 years. These notes are offered and guaranteed by the U.S. Government. They are issued at a discount and pay their full face value at maturity.

TSA (tax-sheltered annuity)

Tax deferred annuity retirement plan available to employees of public schools and colleges, and certain non-profit hospitals, charitable, religious, scientific and educational organizations.

U

Underwriter (banking)

A person, banker or group that guarantees to furnish a definite sum of money by a definite date in return for an issue of bonds or stock.

Underwriter (insurance)

The one assuming a risk in return for the payment of a premium, or the person who assesses the risk and establishes premium rates.

Underwriter (investments)

In the bond/stock market means a brokerage firm or group of firms that has promised to buy a new issue of bonds/shares from a government or company at a fixed discounted price, then arranges to resell them to investors at full price.

Unemployment rate

The number of people unemployed measured as a percentage of the labor force.

Universal life insurance

An adjustable Universal Life insurance policy provides both a death benefit and an investment component called a cash value. The cash value earns interest at rates dictated by the insurer. The policyholder may accumulate significant cash value over the years and, in some circumstances, "borrow" the appreciated funds without paying taxes on the borrowed gains (taxes may be required if policy is surrendered). As long as the policy stays in force the borrowed funds do not need to be repaid, but interest may be charged to your cash value account. Premiums are adjustable by the policy owner.

V

Variable investment

A variable investment is any investment whose value, and therefore returns, fluctuates with market conditions such as a common stock, a plot of raw land, and a hard asset.

Variable universal life insurance

A Variable Life insurance policy provides both a death benefit and an investment component called a cash value. The owner of the policy invests the cash value in sub accounts selected by the insurer. The policyholder may accumulate significant cash value over the years and "borrow" the appreciated funds without paying taxes on the borrowed gains (taxes may be required if policy is surrendered). As long as the policy stays in force the borrowed funds do not need to be repaid, but interest may be charged to your cash value account.

Variable rate mortgage (VRM)

A Variable Rate Mortgage offers an initial interest rate that is usually lower than a fixed rate, but that adjusts periodically according to market conditions and financial indices. The rate may go up and/or down, depending on economic conditions. To limit the borrower's risk, the VRM will almost always have a maximum interest rate allowed, called a "rate cap."

Vesting

Vesting entitles you to the contributions your employer has made to a pension or retirement savings plan for you, including matching contributions to salary reduction plans. You become vested when you have been employed at that job for at least the minimum period the plan requires. Those limits are established by federal law.

Viatical settlement

Occurs when a person with terminal or chronic illness sells his/her life insurance policy to a third party for an amount that is less than the full amount of the death benefit. The buyer becomes the new owner and/ or beneficiary of the life insurance policy, pays all future premiums, and collects the entire death benefit when the insured dies. Some states regulate the purchase as a security while others may regulate it as insurance.

Waiver of premium

A waiver of premium rider on an insurance policy sets for conditions under which premium payments are not required to be made for a time. The most popular waiver of premium rider is the disability waiver under which the owner of the policy (also called the policyholder) is not required to make premium payments during a period of total disability.

Whole life insurance

A traditional Whole Life insurance policy provides both a death benefit and a cash value component. The policy is designed to remain in force for a lifetime. Premiums stay level and the death benefit is guaranteed. Over time, the cash value of the policy grows and helps keep the premium level. Although the premiums start out significantly higher than that of a comparable term life policy, over time the level premium eventually is overtaken by the ever-increasing premium of a term policy.

Will

The most basic and necessary of estate planning tools, a will is a legal document declaring a person's wishes regarding the disposition of their estate. A will ensures that the right people receive the right assets at the right time. If an individual dies without a will they are said to have died intestate.

X

Y

Yield

The yield on an investment is the total proceeds paid from the investment and is calculated as a percentage of the amount invested.

Z

ANNUITY GLOSSARY

A

Accumulation units

The shares of ownership you have in a variable annuity investment portfolio during the period you are saving for retirement. As you pay additional premiums, you buy additional units.

Annuitant

The person who receives income from an annuity. The annuitant's life expectancy is used to figure the initial income amount the annuity pays.

Annuitize

To convert the accumulated value of an annuity into a stream of income, either for one or more life-times or a specific period of time.

Annuity contract

A legal agreement between you and an insurance company, sometimes called an annuity company.

Annuity units

The number of units you own in a variable annuity investment portfolio during the period you are taking income. The number of your annuity units is fixed, and does not change.

Assumed interest rate (AIR)

The rate of interest an annuity provider uses in determining the amount of each variable annuity income payment. Also known as the benchmark rate or the hurdle rate.

Annuity purchase rate

The cost of an annuity based on insurance company tables, which take into account various factors such as your age and gender.

B

C

Commutable contract

An annuity contract that allows you to terminate an annuitization agreement that is paying you income on a fixed period or fixed percentage basis.

Contract value

The combined total of your principal and the portfolio earnings in a variable annuity, up to and including the date on which you annuitize. Also known as accumulate value.

D

Deferred annuity

An annuity contract that you purchase either with a single premium or with periodic payments to help save for retirement. With a deferred annuity, you can choose the point at which you convert the accumulated principal and earning in your contract to a stream of income.

E

Expense ratio

The amount, as a percentage of your total annuity account value that you pay annually for operating, management, and insurance expenses.

F

Fixed annuity

An annuity contract that guarantees you will earn a stated rate of interest during the accumulation phase of a deferred annuity, and that you will receive a fixed amount of income on a regular schedule when you annuitize.

G

Guaranteed death benefit

The assurance that your beneficiaries will receive at least the amount you put into the annuity and typically your locked-in earnings if you die before beginning to take income. This guarantee is one of the insurance benefits that annuities provide.

H

I

Immediate annuity

An annuity contract that you buy with a lump sun and begin to receive income from within a short period, always less than 13 months. An immediate annuity can be either fixed or variable.

Income options

The various methods of receiving annuity income that an annuity contract offers. You may choose from among them the one that suits your situation best. Typically, there are six or more choices, many guaranteeing income for life.

Investment portfolio

A collection of individual investments chosen by a professional manger to produce a clearly defined investment objective. Portfolios, which are structured the same way as open-end mutual funds, are offered in a variable annuity contract and are available to people who purchase the contract. They also are called subaccounts or investment account.

J

K

L

M

Market value adjustment

This feature, which is included in some annuity contracts, imposes an adjustment, or fee, if you surrender your fixed annuity or the fixed account of your variable annuity. The adjustment offsets any losses the insurance company might incur in liquidating assets to pay the amount due to you.

N

Nonqualified annuity

An annuity contract you buy individually rather than as part of an employer sponsored qualified retirement plan. You pay the premium with after-tax dollars. With a deferred nonqualified annuity, your principal grows tax deferred.

O

P

Premium

The amount you pay to buy an annuity or any other insurance product. With a single premium annuity you pay just once, but with other types you pay an initial premium and then make additional premium payments.

Principal

The amount of money you use to purchase an annuity, bond, mutual fund, stock or other investment. The principal is the base on which your earnings accumulate.

Proprietary portfolios

The investment portfolios offered within a variable annuity that are run by the insurance company's investment managers. The annuity may also offer portfolios run by managers working for another financial institution, such as a mutual fund.

Q

Qualified annuity

An annuity contract you buy with pretax dollars as part of an employer-sponsored qualified retirement plan.

R

Rollover

An IRA or qualified retirement plan that you move from one trustee to another is known as a rollover. You can rollover any qualified plan, including a qualified annuity, into an IRA, preserving its tax-deferred status.

S

Separate account

The account established by the insurance company to hold the money you contribute to your variable annuity. It is separate from the company's general account, where fixed annuity premiums are deposited. Money in the separate account is not available to the company's creditors.

Single premium annuity

This type of annuity contract is purchased with a one-time payment. All immediate annuities and some deferred nonqualified annuities are in this category.

Subaccount

The investment portfolios offered in variable annuity contracts are sometimes referred to as subaccounts. The term refers to their position as accounts held within the separate account of the insurance company offering the variable annuity.

T

Tiered interest crediting

A policy used by some companies who credit different interest rates to a fixed annuity's cash surrender value than they do to its annuitization value. This means the interest rate you earn is based on whether you surrender the annuity for cash or annuitize the contract for at least a minimum period and agree to the company's rules about how and when you can access your money. Typically, the rate is significantly higher if you choose the annuitization option. When comparing contracts, it's important to know if the rate you're being quoted applies to the cash surrender value or the annuitization value.

U

Underlying investments

The stocks, bonds, cash equivalents or other investments purchased by a variable annuity portfolio or mutual fund with the money you and other people allocate to that portfolio or fund.

Unit value

The dollar value of a single accumulation or annuity unit, which changes constantly to reflect the current combined total value of the underlying investments in your investment portfolios, minus expenses.

Variable annuity

An annuity contract that allows you to allocate your premium among a number of investment portfolios. Your contract value, which can fluctuate in the short term, reflects the performance of the underlying investments held in those portfolios, minus the contract expenses.

Resources

The following resources will help you make some of the crucial benefit decisions discussed throughout this book:

www.narfe.org

Established in 1921, NARFE works to safeguard and improve the earned rights and benefits of America's active and retired federal employees.

www.federaldaily.com

A leading provider of books, newsletters and other information services to federal employees. They also publish one of the most technical, comprehensive and informative books regarding federal benefits, The Federal Employees Almanac, and it is a must own for all federal employees.

www.usa.gov

Obtain official information and services from the U.S. government...online! They make it easy and offer an abundance of information, services and resources.

www.benefitscheckup.org

Many older people need help paying for prescription drugs, health care, utilities and other basic needs. Ironically, millions of older Americans – especially those with limited incomes – are eligible for but not receiving benefits from existing federal, state and local programs. Ranging from heating and energy assistance to prescription savings programs to income supplements, there are many public programs available to seniors in need if they only knew about them and how to apply for them.

Developed and maintained by the National Council on Aging (NCOA), BenefitsCheckUp is the nation's most comprehensive web-based service to screen for benefits programs for seniors with limited income and resources.

BenefitsCheckUp includes more than 1, 700 public and private benefits programs from all 50 states and the District of Columbia, such as:

- Prescription drugs

- Nutrition (including Supplemental Nutrition Assistance (SNAP)/Food Stamps)

- Energy assistance

- Financial

- Legal

- Health care

- Social Security

- Housing

- In-home services

- Tax relief

- Transportation

- Educational assistance

- Employment

- Volunteer services

Since 2001, millions of people have used BenefitsCheckUp to find benefits programs that help them pay for prescription drugs, health care, rent, utilities, and other needs. For more information on BenefitsCheckUp, contact them at <u>comments@benefitscheckup.org</u>.

For additional information, or to schedule a private consultation concerning your specific situation, please visit our website at www.fedbenefitsgroup.com and fill out the information in the "contact us" section.